GREETING CARDS

for ~~EVERY OCC~~ASION

MaryJo McGraw

NORTH LIGHT BOOKS

CINCINNATI, OHIO

www.artistsnetwork.com

about the author

MaryJo McGraw is a nationally known rubber stamp artist and author whose work has been featured in leading rubber stamp-enthusiast publications. Innovative techniques and creative teaching methods have made her a much sought-after instructor at conventions, retreats, cruises and stores for over 15 years.

Greeting Cards for Every Occasion. Copyright © 2004 by MaryJo McGraw. Manufactured in China. All rights reserved. The patterns and drawings in the book are for personal use of reader. By permission of the author and publisher, they may be either hand-traced or photocopied to make single copies, but under no circumstances may they be resold or republished. It is permissible for the purchaser to make the projects contained herein and sell them at fairs, bazaars and craft shows. No other part of this book may be reproduced in any form or by any electronic or mechanical means including information storage and retrieval systems without permission in writing from the publisher, except by a reviewer, who may quote a brief passage in review. Published by North Light Books, an imprint of F&W Publications, Inc., 4700 East Galbraith Road, Cincinnati, Ohio 45236. (800) 289-0963. First edition.

08 07 06 05 04   5 4 3 2 1

Library of Congress Cataloging-in-Publication Division
McGraw, MaryJo
    Greeting cards for every occasion / with MaryJo McGraw.--1st ed.
        p. cm.
    Includes index.
    ISBN 1-58180-410-5
    1. Greeting cards. I. Title

    TT872.M342 2004
    745.594"1--dc21

                    2003059967

Editor: Krista Hamilton
Designer: Joanna Detz
Layout Artist: Karla Baker
Production Coordinator: Sara Dumford
Photographers: Christine Polomsky and Al Parrish
Stylist: Mary Barnes Clark

Metric Conversion Chart

TO CONVERT	TO	MULTIPLY BY
Inches	Centimeters	2.54
Centimeters	Inches	0.4
Feet	Centimeters	30.5
Centimeters	Feet	0.03
Yards	Meters	0.9
Meters	Yards	1.1
Sq. Inches	Sq. Centimeters	6.45
Sq. Centimeters	Sq. Inches	0.16
Sq. Feet	Sq. Meters	0.09
Sq. Meters	Sq. Feet	10.8
Sq. Yards	Sq. Meters	0.8
Sq. Meters	Sq. Yards	1.2
Pounds	Kilograms	0.45
Kilograms	Pounds	2.2
Ounces	Grams	28.4
Grams	Ounces	0.035

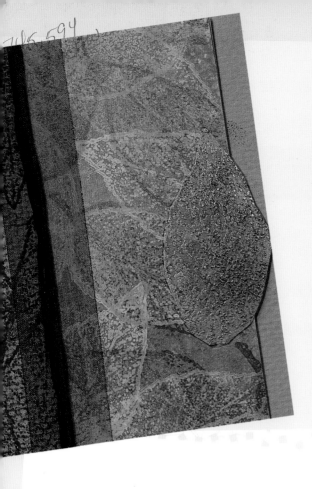

dedication

To all the customers I see

throughout the country

at classes and shows—thanks!

acknowledgments

Thanks to Shirley Hardee and Debra Valoff for their endless encouragement during this particular book. I owe a huge debt of gratitude to my editor, Krista Hamilton, for her tireless effort. Thanks again to the North Light crew for the pure pleasure of working with you guys!

contents

INTRODUCTION, 6

GETTING STARTED, 8

BASIC TOOLS & MATERIALS, 10

BASIC TECHNIQUES [14]

14 How to Hold a Craft Knife

14 How to Hold a Ruler

15 How to Ink a Large Stamp

15 How to Clean Your Stamps

16 How to Score Paper

17 How to Carve a Stamp

18 How to Remove Smudges

19 How to Make a Mask

THE PROJECTS, 20

CARDS FOR WINTER [22]

24 Christmas Box

30 Light the Menorah

34 Joseph's Coat

38 Glazed Metallics

42 Cross My Heart

46 Hearts of Gold

CARDS FOR SPRING [50]

52 Party Gras!

56 Peekaboo Bunny

62 Sunbonnets in Spring

66 A Mother's Love

CARDS FOR SUMMER [68]

70 Facing the Future

74 In the Mail

76 Celebration of Summer

CARDS FOR FALL [80]

82 Spooky Sentiments

86 Gobbler Greetings

90 Fall Foliage

CARDS FOR TIMELESS OCCASIONS [94]

96 Tiny Dancer

100 I Do

104 Bundle of Joy

108 Sweet Celebration

112 Comfy and Cozy

116 Cocktails, Anyone?

120 Home Sweet Home

RESOURCE GUIDE, 124
INDEX, 126

INTRODUCTION

there is no other communication so dear as a sincere greeting card. Whether it is for a holiday, a special event or even just a thoughtful note, a greeting card is like a virtual hug. And a handmade card is even more special! In this day and age, knowing you took the time to create something just for that special someone is heartwarming.

Creating your own greeting cards can be very rewarding. And since the price of an especially nice printed greeting has skyrocketed, it certainly makes sense to create your own. Many cards can be made simply with a few products and papers that can be used over and over. That said, my advice is to buy the best products you can afford. After all, handmade items reflect the person who has created them. Quality shows, and in the long run, it saves time, money and effort when used effectively.

In this book, I have included a variety of creative techniques. You'll find a three-dimensional box card perfect for holding small treats, a Thanksgiving card made with a hand-carved turkey stamp, a pop-up card with a surprise inside and many more. The projects require some common craft supplies like cardstock and craft scissors, and also some supplies that may be new to you, like pewter stickers and acrylic tiles. That's part of the fun! All you need is a little time, a lot of imagination and a quick trip to your favorite stamping supply store. Soon, you'll be on your way to creating greeting cards for every occasion. Enjoy!

getting started

everyone, I think, starts with the belief that they are saving money when they begin to create their own cards. While this is definitely true in the long run, an initial investment must be made on tools and supplies. The real reason for making your own greeting cards is to fulfill your own need to create something wonderful for someone special. Knowing this makes the time and effort you put into a project more precious.

Before you begin, there are a few basic things you need to know for making your own greeting cards. I like to think of these simple techniques as the building blocks. Are they absolutely necessary? No. But doing things properly the first time will make the entire experience much more enjoyable.

Basic Tools & Materials

Tools

There are a few tools that always come in handy when I'm making greeting cards or working on another type of crafting project.

Bone folder

The bone folder is a great tool for scoring paper and smoothing down creases. Bookbinders use it for turning corners and scoring. Some bone folders are actually made from bone as the name suggests, while others are made from resin or wood. They come in a variety of lengths and are very helpful in all kinds of crafts.

Brayer

Brayers come in so many varieties, it's hard to choose which to buy. For my money, the best all-around brayer is the detachable 4" (10cm) soft rubber brayer. It will handle most jobs and is much easier to clean than other brayers. You will also find sponge, acrylic, hard rubber and wooden brayers. Each yields a different result. Try them all and see which one you like the best.

Craft knife

A craft knife is an invaluable tool when creating greeting cards and other stamp projects. X-acto is the most common brand. The blade should be very sharp and should be changed often to ensure clean cuts. You will learn more about the proper way to hold a craft knife on page 14.

Craft scissors

A good pair of stainless steel craft scissors are a must for most craft projects. They should be lightweight and have a comfortable grip for easy maneuverability when cutting out fine details.

Double-stick tape

Double-stick tape comes in a variety of forms and is available at art supply stores. In this book, I have used regular double-stick tape and dimensional double-stick dots.

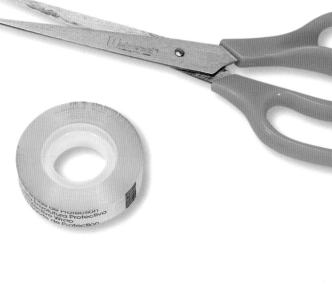

Embellishments

Beautifying your cards with decorative embellishments is the best part about card-making. Browse the aisles of your local craft store and experiment with all the different kinds of paint, markers, crayons, powders, pens and more.

Embossing powder

Embossing powder is required for many of the cards in this book. To use it, stamp an image with pigment or embossing ink. Dust the powder over the wet ink and shake off the excess. Use an embossing tool (heat gun) to melt the powder and create a raised design. Embossing powder comes in metallic, solid and multicolor forms.

Water-soluble crayons

These are available in stamp and art supply stores. I prefer soy-based crayons because they have a creamy texture and are loaded with pigment.

Powdered pigments

These are raw pigments used for a variety of purposes, including making your own paints. You can also use these pigments as a surface coating on paper or collage projects. Powdered pigments do need what is known as a "binder" to keep them adhered to your project. In this book, we will be using Diamond Glaze as a binder. Other options include white glue, paint media, gum arabic or spray fixative. Mix any of these with the powdered pigments to create a colored medium you can apply to many surfaces.

Thread, beads and cords

Decorative accessories such as thread, beads, paper cord, tassels and gift tags can be found at most stamp stores. I also find these items in specialty stores for beads and needlecrafts. Office supply stores are great for unusual items, too. Keep your eyes peeled because you never know what you'll find in the most unlikely places.

Paper

Always buy the best paper you can afford. When I lay out paper for a class, inevitably people choose the most expensive pieces first. Can you guess why? Great paper looks and feels fabulous. Paper is where I spend the bulk of my money every year.

Cardstock

I have used cardstock—a heavy, textured paper—for most of the greeting cards in this book. Cardstock comes in all sorts of colors and textures and is durable enough to withstand a little wear and tear.

Vellum

Vellum is a translucent paper with a smooth finish. It comes in a variety of weights, colors and patterns. Lighter weight vellum is easier to cut and score, but heavier vellum works better for heat embossing and painting.

Acetate

Although acetate is considered a plastic rather than a paper product, it can be used in a similar way as vellum. The clear plastic can be found in most stamp stores. Be sure to get embossable acetate (also known as "window plastic") in case you want to heat the piece. The thicker the laminate, the better it will work for the projects in this book because of the beating the pieces will take.

Stamps

There are millions of stamp designs out there, and again this is the time to invest in quality. I prefer well-trimmed, thick red rubber mounted on wood, or deeply etched unmounted rubber. Foam stamps are great for kids and temporary projects, but as a collector and an artist, I want a stamp that will hold up to use, abuse and time. All of the companies listed in the Resource Guide (pages 124 - 125) make quality stamps.

Ink

When it comes to ink, things can be very confusing. There are so many inks that perform a multitude of tasks, and they are available in every color under the sun! Let me break it down for you.

Dye ink

Most of the time, dye inkpads come with solid lids over the tops. This is because the ink is translucent and you cannot tell what the true color is until it has been stamped. Dye inks work on all types of paper and many porous surfaces. They are best for beginners and produce the most vibrant colors. Most dye inks will fade to some extent, and they tend to dry quickly, making them a poor choice for embossing. This also means dye inkpads can dry out quickly if you live in a dry climate.

Pigment ink

Slower-drying pigment ink is opaque and resembles paint. This ink is used for embossing or foiling with dry pigments. It is best suited for porous, uncoated paper. There are several brands, such as Brilliance, that dry on shiny and slick paper, but it takes a long time. To speed up the process, dry pigment inks with an embossing tool (heat gun). Since pigment inks are opaque, many are metallic or pearlized.

Solvent ink

Solvent ink, also called permanent ink, is made specifically for nonporous surfaces, but it also works well on paper. When dry, solvent ink does not smear—even when water is applied—making it perfect for watercolor techniques and markers. Since solvent ink works on every surface, it is my personal favorite.

Here is my basic advice: If you have never bought a single inkpad, buy a dye inkpad, a pigment inkpad and a solvent inkpad—each one in black. Then, buy your favorite metallic (gold, silver, copper or bronze) color in pigment ink and ten good colors of dye ink. These supplies should see you through most projects. After that, you are on your own in this addiction to color! I still buy almost every color of most of the brands out there.

Basic Techniques

There are a few basic techniques you'll need to know before you begin. These little tricks, which I've picked up over the years, will make every project easier and more enjoyable.

How to Hold a Craft Knife

The best way to make precise cuts with a craft knife is to control your blade. A sharp blade is also important, so be sure to replace it often.

1. Position the Knife
Hold the craft knife like a pencil and point the blade straight down toward the paper.

2. Make the Cut
Push the point of the blade into the surface, and then pull it down as far as you can, holding the blade parallel to the surface as you cut.

How to Hold a Ruler

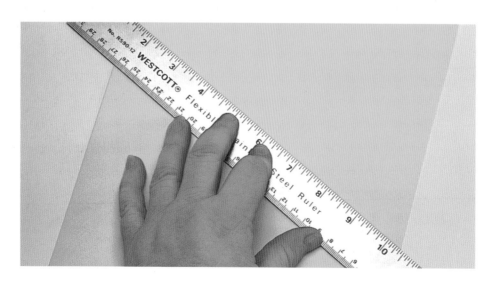

Holding your ruler correctly will make all the difference between a good card and a great card. Follow this technique and see for yourself!

Position the Ruler
Hold the ruler with your ring finger and thumb firmly positioned on the outside edge. This will prevent the ruler from slipping. Place your index and middle fingers directly on the ruler.

How to Ink a Large Stamp

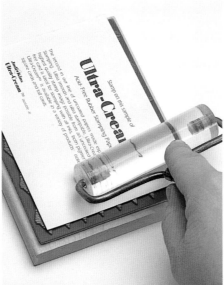

Nothing is more frustrating than lifting the stamp from your paper, only to find half the image didn't transfer. You must be sure to ink your stamp properly, especially when using large stamps like some of the ones in this book. Keep trying. In the stamping world, you get plenty of chances to make a good impression.

1. Ink Stamp

For the best coverage, rub the surface of the stamp with a pad of ink.

2. Transfer Image

Keeping the stamp facing up, position the cardstock on the stamp and roll a soft rubber brayer over the back of the cardstock to transfer the image.

How to Clean Your Stamps

When cleaning your stamps, use a cleaner with conditioner in it. I prefer a solvent-type cleaner, which removes any ink or paint I might be using. I personally do not like to overclean my stamps. This can damage the cushion under the die and loosen the adhesive.

1. Apply Cleaner

Apply a generous amount of stamp cleaner to the rubber stamp.

2. Blot Stamp

Blot the stamp on a clean, dry paper towel and reuse as necessary or store.

How to Score Paper

Scoring is especially important on heavy cardstock. Many tools can be used, such as a bone folder, paper clip, ballpoint pen, stylus or the back of a craft knife. Using your ruler as a guide, press down hard to get a nice, crisp crease.

Score with Craft Knife
For a sharp crease, score with the back of a craft knife.

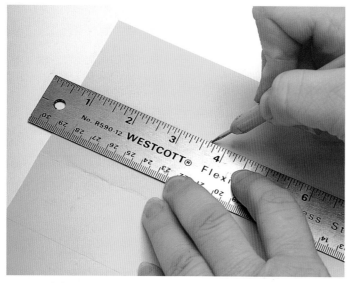

Score with a Stylus
For a soft crease, score with a stylus.

Always Use Tools
Never crease the paper by hand to score it.

TIP

For the most impressive pop-up and tri-fold cards, crisp scoring is a must!

How to Carve a Stamp

Carving your own designs into rubber is fun and addictive! Stamp carving tools are available in a variety of tip sizes, ranging from extremely thin to extremely wide. Soft white or pink rubber erasers work best for carving. You can even order large carving blocks up to 4' x 6' (123cm x 183cm) if you really get into it!

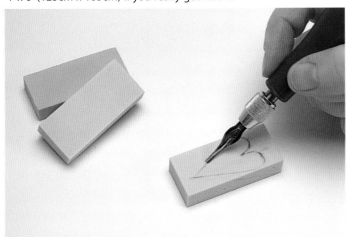

1. Draw and Trace Design
Draw your design in pencil on a soft rubber eraser. Trace the outline of the design with a thin carving tool.

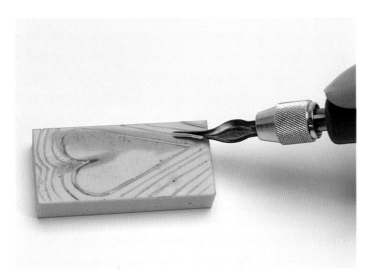

3. Carve Stamp
Carve around the stamped image with carving tools. Remove large chunks with a wide tip, and carve fine details with a thin tip.

2. Ink Stamp
Ink the stamp and stamp it onto paper. This will indicate the areas that still need to be carved and cleaned up.

4. Ink Stamp
Ink the stamp and stamp it onto paper again.

How to Carve a Stamp (cont.)

5. Cut Away Excess
Cut away the unwanted portions of the eraser with the craft knife.

6. Stamp onto Paper
Stamp the inked image onto paper again to test it out.

How to Remove Smudges

We all make mistakes from time to time. It's part of the learning process. Accidental smudge marks can be easily fixed with a regular craft knife and a white eraser.

1. Scrape Paper
Using your craft knife, gently scrape the surface of the paper over the error. Be careful not to tear the paper.

2. Erase Rest
Rub the area with a white eraser to remove the rest of the smudge.

How to Make a Mask

Masking is an important technique to master, and practice makes perfect! In regular masking, the mask covers up the object, and the images are stamped around it. For an example of regular masking, see "In the Mail" on page 74. In mortise masking, the area around the object is masked, and the object itself is stamped. For an example of mortise masking, see "Comfy and Cozy" on page 112. Try both and see which technique you like best.

Many crafters use Post-it notes for masking because they are lightly adhesive and available in many sizes. I prefer Eclipse tape by JudiKins, and have used it for the projects in this book. This product is sold by the roll and is lightly adhesive on one side.

1. Stamp on Eclipse Tape
Ink a stamp and roll Eclipse tape over it.

2. Cut Out Eclipse Tape
Cut out the portion of the stamped Eclipse tape you want to mask off. For a regular mask, use the object itself. For a mortise mask, use the area around the object.

3. Stamp Paper
Stamp the paper with colored inkpads.

4. Ink and Stamp
Ink a stamp with colored ink and stamp over the colors on the paper. Remove the mask to reveal a stamped card.

THE PROJECTS

now that you know the basics of card-making, you're ready to begin. The cards in this book are broken into five categories: Winter, Spring, Summer, Fall and Timeless Occasions. As you follow my step-by-step instructions, feel free to use your own stamps, colors and materials, and try not to limit yourself by the season. By swapping out a few stamps and a piece of cardstock, the Christmas Box card can easily become a tiny box to hold wedding favors. I hope you use the techniques shown in each project as a springboard for more fun and creative ideas. Remember, there is no right or wrong way to make a handmade greeting card. The more personalized it is, the better!

CARDS FOR WINTER

Winter is the time of year when families and friends get together to celebrate holidays and special occasions. What a perfect opportunity to create greetings that will make them glow with delight. I can think of nothing better than curling up by the fire on a cold winter's night with only my card-making supplies and my creativity. A simple, handmade greeting card may be the small gift that warms the heart of someone you love this season.

SPREAD HOLIDAY CHEER WITH THESE WINTER CARDS:

Christmas Box 24 Light the Menorah 30 Joseph's Coat 34 Glazed Metallics 38

Cross My Heart 42 Hearts of Gold 46

CHRISTMAS BOX

This is a simple and fun card to make for many holidays. The three-dimensional box can be filled with candy, small toys, gift certificates or money, which makes it perfect for Christmas or Hanukkah! There are many template stamps like this one available at your local stamp store.

TIP

This is an easy card to replicate over and over if taken in steps. I make holiday cards in bulk, completing one step each night. That way, I stay focused and get several cards done at once!

What you'll Need

Stamps*

- Box template stamp
- Present stamp
- Christmas tree stamp

Materials

- 3 pieces of green cardstock
- White cardstock
- Clear acetate square
- Black dye ink
- Red dye ink
- Green dye ink
- Clear-drying glue
- Glitter
- Double-stick tape
- Craft scissors
- Craft knife
- Ruler

See Resource Guide for stamp credits.

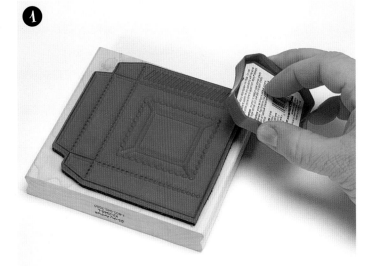

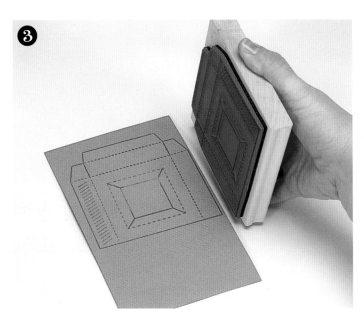

1. Ink Outside of Box Template Stamp
Ink the outside edge of the box template stamp with black dye ink.

2. Stamp on Cardstock
Stamp it onto two separate pieces of green cardstock. One will be the back of the box (panel A) and the other will be the door panel (panel B) that covers the card.

3. Ink and Stamp Inside of Box Template
Ink the entire box template stamp and stamp it onto another piece of green cardstock. This becomes the front of the box that has the picture frame (panel C).

4. Stamp Gift Image

Ink the present stamp and randomly stamp it on the blank side of the panel A with red dye ink. Repeat with panels B and C.

5. Cut Out Box Outline

Cut out the box shapes with craft scissors.

6. Remove Extra Panel

On panel B, cut off the two extra flaps, leaving a single flap to glue on the box.

7. Cut Out Box Center

Cut out the center of panel C with a craft knife.

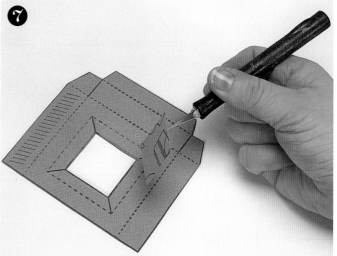

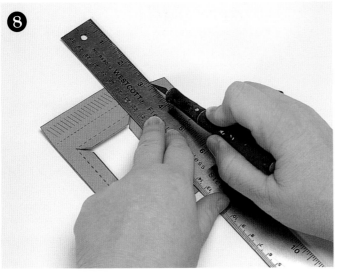

8. Score Along Dotted Lines
Using the back of a craft knife, score along the dotted lines on each panel.

9. Tape Down Frame
Tape down the inside window frame of panel C This gives a much more finished edge to the inside rim of the frame.

10. Add Acetate Square
Cut out a square of clear acetate and adhere it to the inside of panel C with clear-drying glue. Set aside.

11. Ink and Stamp Christmas Tree Image
Ink the Christmas tree stamp with green dye ink and stamp it on white cardstock.

For a stained glass effect, try using colored acetate!

12. Add Glue
Add dots of clear-drying glue around the tree.

13. Add Glitter "Snow"
Sprinkle the wet glue with a generous amount of glitter to create the look of snow. Wipe away the excess.

14. Trim Cardstock
Trim the white cardstock to fit inside the frame.

15. Assemble Box
Attach panel A to panel C with double-stick tape.

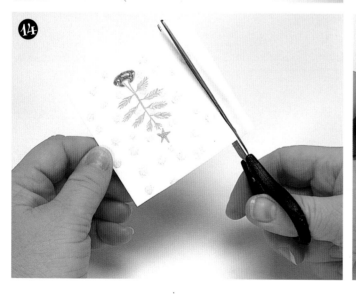

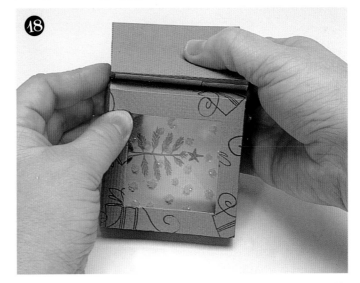

16. Arrange Flaps
Be sure the side flaps on panel C are positioned on the outside of the box.

17. Tape Box Shut
Adhere a strip of double-stick tape to the flap that will be tucked into the box to hold it closed.

NOTE: If you plan to put candy in the box, skip step 17.

18. Attach Door
Adhere a strip of double-stick tape to the small flap on panel B and attach it to the side of the box.

19. Bend Door to Open and Close
Bend panel B back and forth a few times to make sure it opens and closes properly. What a nice Christmas surprise!

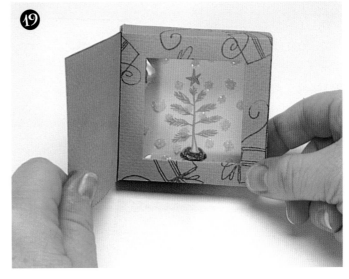

LIGHT THE MENORAH

acrylic paints are great for card-making because they layer well, are lightweight and clean up with water. These pearlized acrylic paints are gorgeous when applied to richly colored paper. For a softer, smoother finish, try using a cosmetic sponge instead of a stiff brush to apply the paint. Be sure the paint is completely dry before embossing so the powder sticks only to the image.

TIP

Edging this card with the same silver color as the embossing powder will really light up this Menorah!

What you'll Need

Stamps*

- Decorative stamp
- Menorah stamp

Materials

- 2 pieces of white cardstock
- Folded silver greeting card
- Dark blue acrylic paint
- Light blue acrylic paint
- Navy blue pigment ink
- Silver pigment ink
- Silver paint pen
- Stiff brush or cosmetic sponge
- Double-stick tape

*See Resource Guide for stamp credits.

1. Apply Dark Blue Acrylic Paint
Generously apply dark blue acrylic paint to a piece of white cardstock with a stiff brush or cosmetic sponge.

2. Apply Light Blue Pigment Paint
Apply light blue acrylic paint to a separate piece of white cardstock.

3. Ink and Stamp Decorative Image
Ink the decorative image with navy blue pigment ink. Stamp along the bottom of the dark blue cardstock.

4. Ink and Stamp Menorah Image

Ink the Menorah stamp with silver pigment ink and stamp it onto the light blue cardstock.

5. Tear Card

Tear the top and bottom of the light blue cardstock to create jagged edges.

6. Outline Cards

Outline the edges of both cards with a silver paint pen.

7. Adhere to Greeting Card

Using double-stick tape, adhere the dark blue layer to the front of a folded silver greeting card. Next, adhere the light blue layer over the dark blue layer.

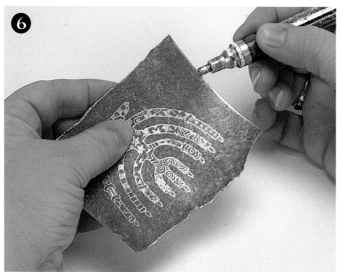

MORE BRIGHT IDEAS

Butterfly in the Sky

I wanted this majestic butterfly to look like it was emerging from the foliage, so I stamped the butterfly first and used paints and powders to decorate it. Then, I stamped the leaves, with metallic paint, over parts of the butterfly to set it back, behind the leaves.

Leaving an Impression

For this card, I stamped the leaves with dark acrylic paint on the card. Then, I layered a piece of cardstock stamped with lighter acrylic paints over it. The cord and ribbon hide the seam where the two pieces meet.

JOSEPH'S COAT

this festive card is great for ringing in the New Year—or any time of year! If you think back to kindergarten, you might remember using this resist method with crayons and black poster paint. While the end result might look a little more sophisticated, the technique is just as simple.

TIP

The closer and thinner you make the lines, the better this technique looks!

What you'll Need

Stamp*

* Nile flowers stained glass stamp

Materials

* White cardstock
* Silver paper
* Folded white greeting card
* Black solvent ink
* Black dye ink
* Black permanent marker
* Colored pencils
* Craft knife
* Craft scissors
* Craft glue
* Paper towels

*See Resource Guide for stamp credits.

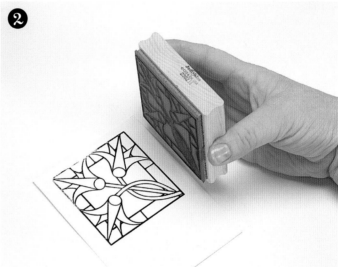

1. Sharpen Colored Pencil
Using a craft knife, sharpen several colored pencils.

2. Ink and Stamp Decorative Image
Ink the Nile flowers stained glass stamp with black solvent ink and stamp onto white cardstock.

3. Color in the Design
Fill in the white spaces of the image with colored pencils. You may color areas solidly or use loose lines to fill in portions of the design like I've done here.

4. Finish Adding Color
Finalize the colored pencil work, adding as much or as little color as you desire.

5. Cover with Dye Ink
Stamp black dye ink over the entire image.

6. Wipe Away Ink
Before the black ink dries, quickly wipe it away with a paper towel. The ink will adhere to all the areas not covered with colored pencil.

7. Trim Cardstock
Trim the sides of the cardstock with craft scissors.

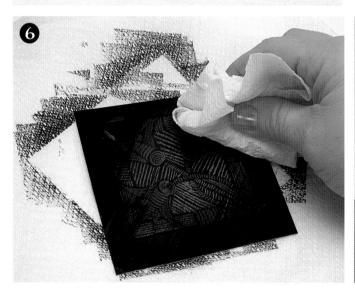

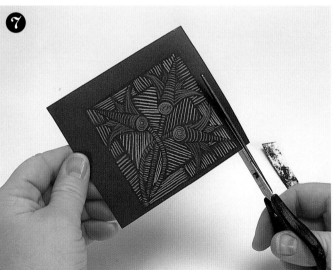

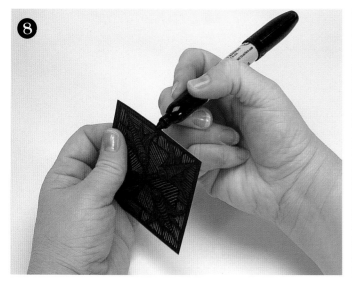

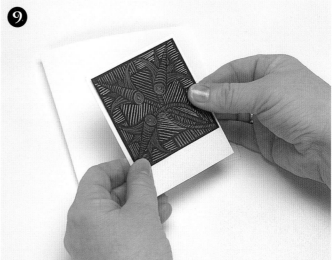

8. Outline Edges
Outline the edges of the cardstock with a black permanent marker.

9. Adhere Cardstock to Paper
Attach the cardstock to a slightly larger piece of silver paper with craft glue, leaving space at the bottom for a message if desired.

10. Attach to Greeting Card
Attach the stamped cardstock and silver paper to a folded white greeting card with craft glue.

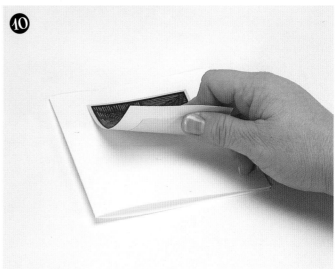

GLAZED METALLICS

i have used this technique for many years to achieve a soft metallic finish on paper. It is great to try over an image that did not emboss well or one that is splotchy. High-quality pigment inks and paper make all the difference when crafting your own cards. For best results, I recommend using Encore brand pigment ink.

TIP

The pewter sticker on this card adds a fancy touch. To learn more about pewter stickers, see the Celebration of Summer card on page 76.

What you'll Need

Stamp*

- Swirl stamp

Materials

- White cardstock
- Folded blue greeting card
- Pewter sticker
- Silver pigment ink (Encore)
- Silver embossing powder
- Red, green and blue dye re-inkers
- Embossing tool (heat gun)
- Craft scissors
- Double-stick tape
- Paper towels

*See Resource Guide for stamp credits.

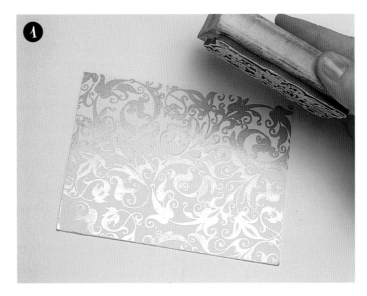

1. Ink and Stamp Decorative Image

Ink the swirl stamp with silver pigment ink (Encore) and stamp onto white cardstock.

2. Add Embossing Powder

Sprinkle silver embossing powder over the ink, then tap the edge of the card to remove the excess powder.

3. Heat-Set Powder

Heat-set the powder with an embossing tool to melt it.

4. Cover Image
Use the same silver stamp pad to stamp all over the cardstock, completely covering the image.

5. Spread Ink with Finger
Rub the silver pigment ink into the surface of the card with your finger.

6. Add Dye
Squeeze a few drops of blue dye from a dye re-inker into a small dish. With your finger, smooth out the ink so it is fairly thin.

7. Buff Image
Buff the image with your inky finger so the dye sticks to the recessed areas. Continue buffing with red and green dye or the colors of your choice.

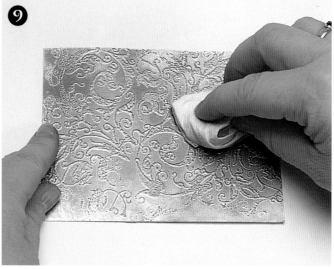

8. Heat-Set Dye
Heat-set the ink and dye with an embossing tool.

9. Buff Cardstock and Adhere to Greeting Card
Buff the cardstock with a paper towel to remove excess ink and dye. Trim the cardstock with craft scissors and adhere to a folded blue greeting card with double-stick tape. Add a pewter sticker for a finishing touch.

 *Try this!*

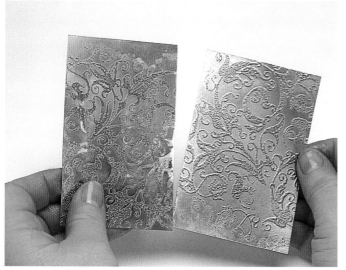

For a rougher look, shown on the left, rub vigorously with a paper towel and/or scrape with a craft knife to remove dye. For a softer look, shown on the right, simply use the buffing technique explained above.

CROSS MY HEART

in February, after the rush of the winter holidays, I am ready to create a few fun valentines with this tricky old pop-up inside. Be sure to add lots of confetti to the cards and send them in brightly colored envelopes. (Sealed with a kiss, of course.)

TIP

Be careful not to go overboard on your colors. For a simple and visually appealing look, I recommend choosing no more than three colors.

What you'll Need

Stamps*

- Hand-carved heart stamp (template on page 44)
- "Happy Valentine's Day" stamp

Materials

- Heart pocket template (page 45)
- Translucent white vellum
- Folded white greeting card
- Bright construction paper
- Dye ink, various colors
- Pencil
- Eraser
- Carving tools
- Double-stick tape
- Decorative paper punch
- Stylus
- Craft scissors or craft knife

*See Resource Guide for stamp credits.

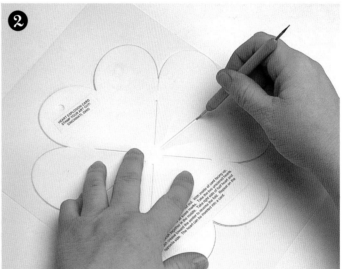

1. Cut and Trace Heart Pocket
Cut out and enlarge the heart pocket template provided on page 45. Trace the outline and score marks of the template onto a piece of translucent vellum with a pencil.

2. Score Template
Score inside the slits with a stylus. Cut out the template with craft scissors or a craft knife.

3. Clean Up Vellum
Erase any pencil marks remaining on the vellum.

4. Crease Vellum

Crease the vellum along the score marks to make the heart pocket. The creases down the center of each heart should fold to the inside.

5. Stamp Images on Vellum

Carve a heart stamp using the template provided below (For carving instructions, see page 17). Randomly stamp the heart and "Happy Valentine's Day" stamps onto the inside of the heart pocket in various colors of dye ink.

6. Stamp Heart Image on Greeting Card

Stamp more hearts onto the outside of a folded white greeting card in various colors.

7. Position Heart Pocket in Greeting Card

Fold the heart pocket back into shape and place it inside the greeting card. Try closing the card to make sure it is in the correct position.

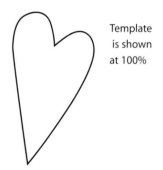

Template is shown at 100%

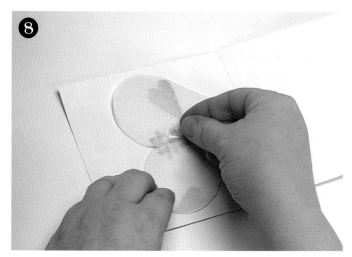

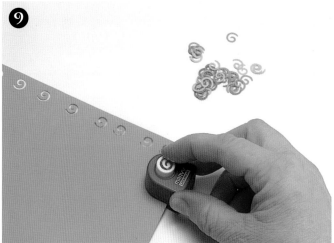

8. Adhere Heart Pocket
Adhere the heart pocket to the inside of the white greeting card with double-stick tape.

9. Punch Out Confetti
Use a decorative paper punch on bright construction paper to make colorful confetti.

10. Add Confetti
Open the card slightly, pour in the confetti, and carefully re-close the card.

Enlarge heart pocket template by 200%, then by 125%.

TIP

Add glitter to the inside of the heart for a shiny (and messy) touch.

HEARTS OF GOLD

this is a creative method of making vivid backgrounds for simple stamps. With a few dye inkpads and a stiff brush for applying color, you can count on getting brilliant results every time! The torn-edge background adds a modern flair and works exceptionally well for underwater or sunset themes.

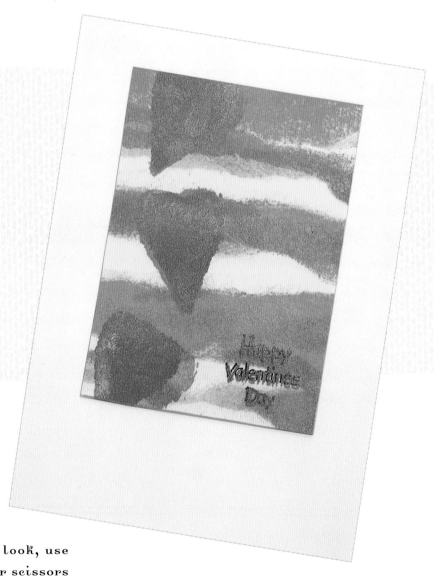

TIP

For a more uniform look, use decorative or regular scissors to cut the Eclipse tape.

What you'll Need

Stamps*

- Heart stamp
- "Happy Valentine's Day" stamp

Materials

- White cardstock
- Folded white greeting card
- Dye ink, various colors
- Gold pigment powder
- Eclipse tape
- Stiff brush
- Craft scissors

See Resource Guide for stamp credits.

1. Mask Background
Tear off thin strips of Eclipse tape and adhere them to a piece of white cardstock to mask portions of the background.

2. Apply Dye Ink
Brush colored dye ink onto the cardstock and over the masks with a stiff brush. Remove and reposition the masks until the desired look is achieved.

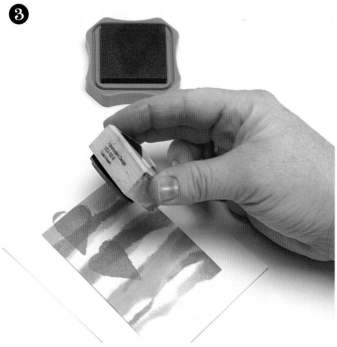

3. Ink and Stamp Heart Image
Ink the heart stamp with pink dye ink and stamp randomly onto the cardstock.

4. Ink and Stamp "Happy Valentine's Day"
Ink the "Happy Valentine's Day" stamp with black dye ink and stamp it onto the bottom right corner.

5. Add Pigment Powder and Adhere to Greeting Card
Dust with gold pigment powder and wipe away the excess. The powder will stick to the wet ink on the hearts and text. Trim the edges and adhere to a white greeting card.

MORE BRIGHT IDEAS

Tie-Dyed Flowers

Torn edges add dimension to cards such as this colorful creation. Hold a piece of paper (cardstock works best) against a flat surface with one hand and slowly tear the paper with the other. Voila!

Midas' Golden Touch

The shimmer of gold cardstock shines through on this card. Don't worry about tearing the edges in a straight line. The more jagged the tear, the better.

CARDS FOR SPRING

after a long winter, the bright colors of spring are like a breath of fresh air! These spring cards are filled with the vibrant colors of a season in bloom. Flowers and nature themes always make great cards for Easter and Mother's Day, but don't forget to keep your eyes open for fun and festive Mardi Gras imagery as well.

WATCH SMILES GROW WITH THESE SPRING CARDS:

Party Gras! 52 Peekaboo Bunny 56 Sunbonnets in Spring 62 A Mother's Love 66

PARTY GRAS!

these days, you don't have to go to New Orleans to celebrate Mardi Gras. This extravaganza of crazy costumes and delectable delights is an excellent time to create a special card, no matter where you happen to live. The mix of creative patterns and vivid colors will whisk you away to The Big Easy, where you'll toss your troubles aside and just have fun!

TIP

To decorate your card in true Mardi Gras fashion, use the official colors of the festival: purple represents justice; green represents faith; and gold represents power.

What you'll Need

Stamps*

* Box template stamp
* Minstrel stamp

Materials

* 2 sheets of decorative paper
* White paper
* Acetate square
* Folded dark blue greeting card
* Black solvent ink
* Silver paint pen
* Colored pencils
* Glitter
* Double-stick tape
* Scoring tool
* Craft scissors or craft knife
* Ruler

See Resource Guide for stamp credits.

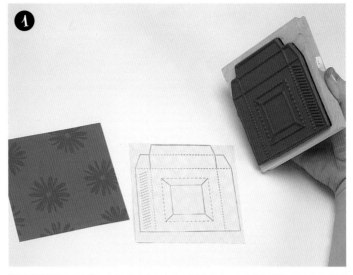

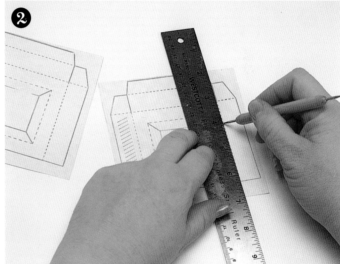

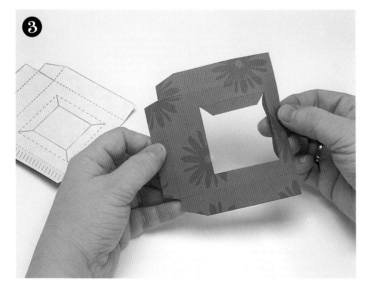

1. Cut and Stamp Decorative Paper

Cut two thin pieces of decorative paper to approximately 3" (7.6cm) square. Stamp the plain sides of each piece of paper with the box template stamp.

2. Score Paper

On one of the pieces of paper, score the outside lines and the window of the box with a stylus. This will be the frame. On the other piece of paper, score only the outside of the box. This will be the back panel for the frame. Cut out both shapes with scissors or a craft knife.

3. Fold Box

Fold the frame along the score marks.

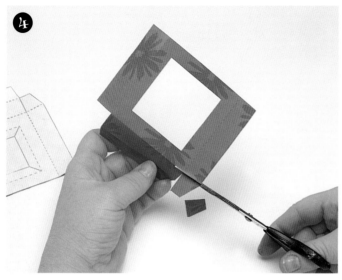

4. Remove Top Flaps

Cut off the little box flaps and bottom flap of the frame with craft scissors.

5. Remove Back Flaps

Trim off all flaps but one from the back panel piece.

6. Remove Top of Flap

Cut the top portion off of the remaining flap on the back panel piece, leaving a single tab.

7. Add Acetate Window

Cut a small square of acetate approximately 2½" x 2½" (6.4cm x 6.4cm) for the frame's window. Adhere the acetate with double-stick tape on the inside of the frame. Attach the remaining back panel flap to the inside of the frame as shown. Be sure the decorative paper is showing through the frame.

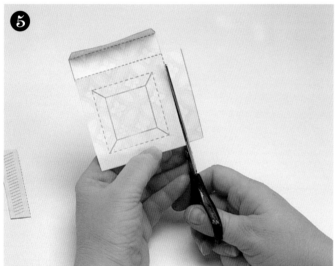

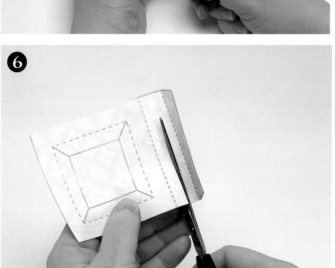

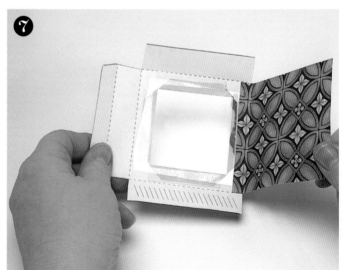

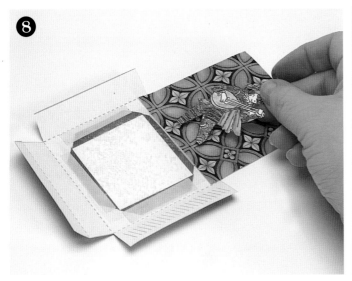

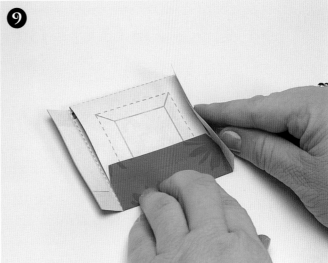

8. Add Minstrel Image

Stamp the minstrel image onto white paper using black solvent ink. Cut it out and decorate it with colored pencils. Place the image in the center of the back panel and add glitter to the window. Fold the frame over the back panel.

9. Fold Flaps

Fold the remaining flaps from the frame in and secure with double-stick tape. Edge the frame with a silver paint pen.

10. Adhere Box to Greeting Card

Use double-stick tape to fasten the decorative framed piece a folded dark blue greeting card.

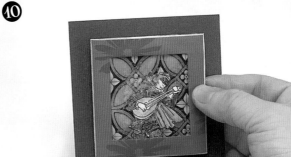

PEEKABOO BUNNY

Whimsy meets whiskers in this Easter card, made just for a special little girl or boy. Tuck it into an Easter basket along with some colored eggs. To take this card a step further, glue Easter grass to the bottom of the card and add a small pink button for the bunny's nose.

TIP

This tri-fold method can also be used for other cards, so don't limit yourself to this design alone.

What you'll Need

Stamps*

- Swirl stamp
- Hand-carved Easter egg stamp (template on page 61)
- Hand-carved bunny face stamps (template on page 61)

Materials

- Bunny body template (page 61)
- Light yellow cardstock
- Vellum or tracing paper
- Blue solvent ink
- Dye ink, various colors
- Pencil
- Eraser
- Carving tools
- Craft knife
- Craft scissors
- Ruler

*See Resource Guide for stamp credits.

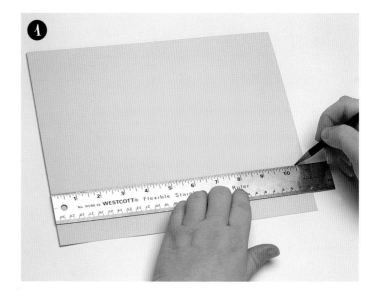

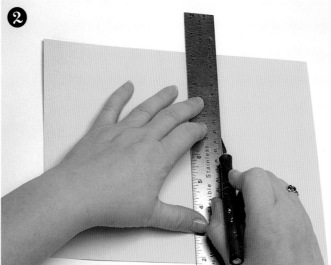

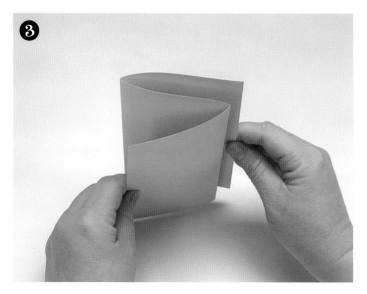

1. Mark Cardstock
Measure 3" (7.6cm), 7" (18cm) and 10" (25cm) and mark with a pencil on light yellow cardstock.

2. Score Cardstock
Score along the 3" (7.6cm) and 7" (18cm) marks with the back of a craft knife or a scoring tool. Erase any remaining pencil marks.

3. Tri-Fold Card
Fold the left panel to the back and the right panel to the front. This is called a tri-fold.

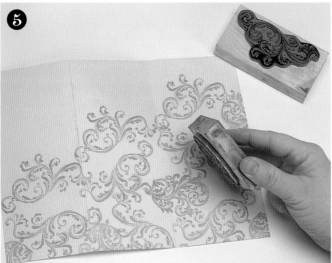

4. Ink and Stamp Swirls

Ink a swirl stamp with blue solvent ink. Flatten out the card and begin stamping the front about one-third of the way up on the left edge. Work your way upward and diagonally to the right edge of the page.

5. Fill Open Spaces

Re-ink the stamp and randomly stamp in between the open spaces of the yellow cardstock to fill in any gaps.

6. Trim Card

Use your craft knife to trim off the top of the card along the stamped edge.

7. Stamp Back of Card

Flip the card over and stamp randomly along the top edges with the swirl stamp.

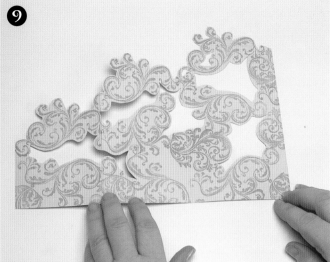

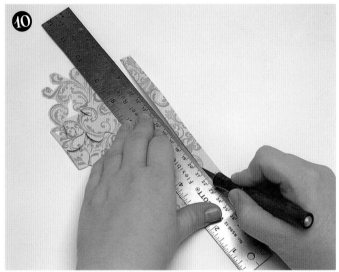

8. Fill Open Spaces

Fill the open spaces on the edges with more stamping.

9. Cut Out Random Pieces

Use your craft knife to cut out random bits and pieces from the inside of the card.

10. Trim Card

Using your ruler as a guide, trim the edges of the card with a craft knife.

11. Ink and Stamp Easter Egg Image

Carve an Easter egg stamp using the template on page 61. (For carving instructions, see page 17). Ink the stamp with colorful dye ink and stamp a border along the bottom of both sides.

Many Easter egg stamps can be found in your local stamping supply store if you don't wish to carve your own.

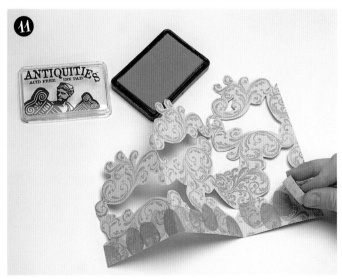

12. Cut Out Bunny Template

Cut out the bunny template provided on page 61. Position the straight side of the template against a folded piece of vellum or tracing paper and trace with a pencil. Cut out the bunny shape.

13. Add Bunny Eyes and Nose

Dip a pencil eraser in pink dye ink and use it to dot the bunny's eyes. Use a small triangular piece of eraser to make a nose, and stamp it with pink dye ink.

14. Add Bunny Ears

Use the template on page 61 to carve the ear shape from an eraser. Stamp it inside each of the bunny's ears with pink dye ink. Poke the bunny's head through holes in the back of the card.

TEMPLATES

Bunny template

Enlarge by 133%

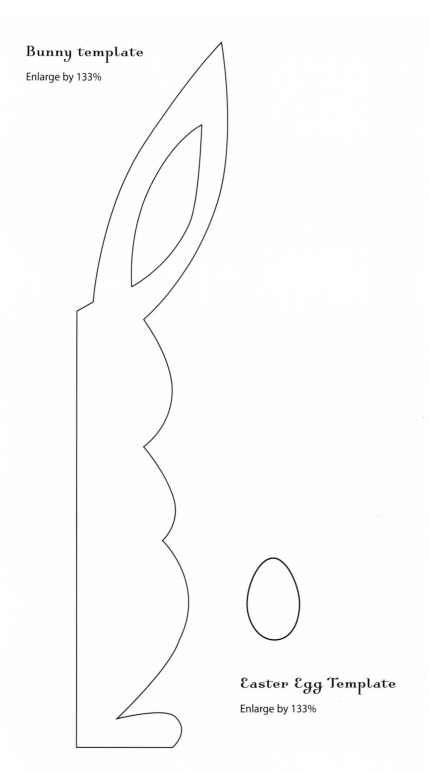

Easter Egg Template

Enlarge by 133%

sunbonnets in spring

here is a favorite trick of mine! The lamp stamps I used here don't have anything to do with spring, but with a little imagination and clever masking, they're transformed into bonnets! Take a good look at your stamps and try to imagine what else they could be. Who knows what you'll dream up!

TIP

This process works better when using different kinds of ink, or at least drastically different colors.

What you'll Need

Stamps*

- Dress stamp
- Chinese lantern stamp
- Lamps stamp

Materials

- White paper
- White cardstock
- Folded white greeting card
- Dye ink, various colors
- Silver dye ink
- Turquoise paint pen
- Eclipse tape
- Double-stick tape
- Craft scissors

*See Resource Guide for stamp credits.

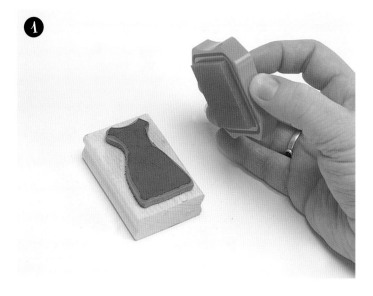

1. Ink Dress Image
Ink the surface of the dress stamp generously with orange dye ink.

2. Ink and Stamp Lantern Image
Ink the Chinese lantern stamp with silver dye ink and stamp the image onto the solid dress stamp to create designs on the dress.

3. Stamp Inked Dress Image
Stamp the dress image onto white paper.

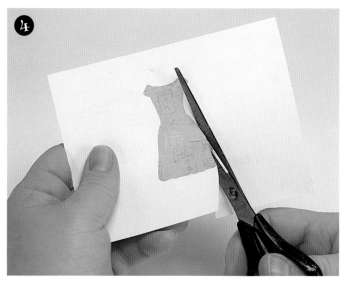

4. Cut Out Dresses
Cut out the dress image with craft scissors. Repeat this process two more times using different colors.

5. Ink and Stamp Lamp Image
Ink the lamp stamp with various brightly colored dye inks and stamp the top of a piece of white cardstock.

6. Mask and Stamp Lamp Bases
Mask off the center of the white cardstock with Eclipse tape and stamp the cardstock again with the lamp image. Only the lamp bases should show up on the cardstock.

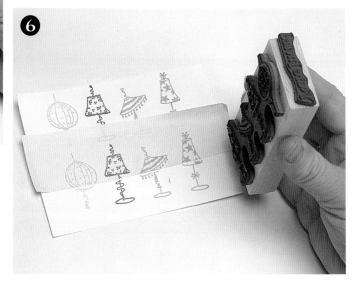

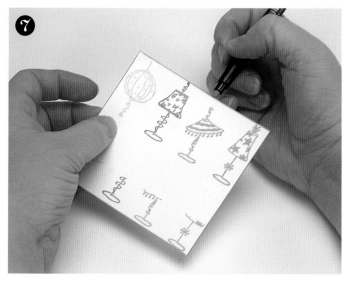

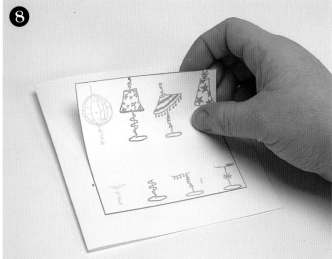

7. Trim Cardstock and Outline Edges

Trim the sides of the cardstock to make it square. Outline the edges with a turquoise paint pen.

8. Adhere Cardstock to Greeting Card

Fasten the square cardstock onto a folded white greeting card with double-stick tape.

9. Adhere Dresses Over Lamp Bases

Adhere the cut-out dresses over the lamp bottoms with double-stick tape.

A MOTHER'S LOVE

m om always appreciates a beautiful card—particularly one made by you! Creating a special card just for her will give you the chance to express your love in a way a store-bought card never could. Use her favorite colors and themes. Add a personal embellishment or an old photograph she will recognize. This is your opportunity to show your mom how much you have appreciated her all these years.

TIP

Galaxy markers are great for coloring in stamped images on light or dark paper. They are available in bright and pastel colors, metallics and glitters, and with fine, medium and broad tips.

What you'll Need

Stamp*

- Triple heart stamp

Materials

- Black solvent ink
- Pink dye ink
- Markers (Galaxy)
- Folded white greeting card

*See Resource Guide for stamp credits.

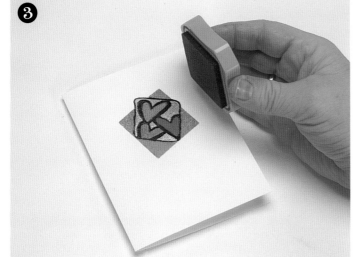

1. Ink and Stamp Heart Image
Ink the triple heart stamp with black solvent ink and stamp it onto the front of a folded white greeting card.

2. Decorate Hearts
Color in the hearts with markers (I use Galaxy brand) and allow the ink to dry.

3. Stamp Over Hearts
Use a pink dye inkpad to stamp over the triple heart image in the opposite direction.

CARDS FOR SUMMER

Summer cards are the forgotten greetings. Between vacations, soccer practice and swimming lessons, who has time for another project? But that doesn't mean there aren't many special events to celebrate, like Graduation, Father's Day and Summer Solstice. Card-making can be done virtually anywhere! A blanket, a cool glass of lemonade and your card supplies are all you need.

MAKE A SPLASH WITH THESE SUMMER CARDS:

Facing the Future 70 In the Mail 74 Celebration of Summer 76

FACING THE FUTURE

graduation is one of life's most cherished moments. Show your favorite grad how much he means to you with a special handmade greeting card. This one can be customized with the grad's school colors. Be sure to leave space for a personalized message (and perhaps a little spending money!).

TIP

Fill in the blank spaces of stamped images to give your cards a more polished look. I use thicker Galaxy markers to color in larger areas and gel pens for smaller, more detailed areas.

What you'll Need

Stamps*

- Large frame stamp
- Small frame stamp
- David stamp

Materials

- Blue cardstock
- Folded blue greeting card
- Black solvent ink
- White marker
- White gel pen
- Double-stick dots
- Craft scissors
- Craft knife

*See Resource Guide for stamp credits.

1. Stamp Frame Images

Cut the blue cardstock into two pieces, a larger one measuring about 4" x 6" (10.2cm x 15.2cm) and a smaller one measuring about 3" x 3½" (7.6cm x 8.9cm). Using black solvent ink, stamp the larger card with the large frame stamp and the smaller card with the small frame stamp.

2. Color in Open Spaces

Fill in all open spaces of the stamped frames with a white marker (I used Galaxy brand) and gel pen.

3. Trim Card Edges

Trim around the edges of both frames with craft scissors.

4. Cut Out Window
Cut out the inside window of the small frame with a craft knife.

5. Stamp and Color David Image
Stamp the David image onto a separate piece of blue cardstock and color in larger areas with a white marker.

6. Fill in Open Spaces
Fill in smaller areas with a white gel pen. For added detail, make tiny dots of gel pen on the face.

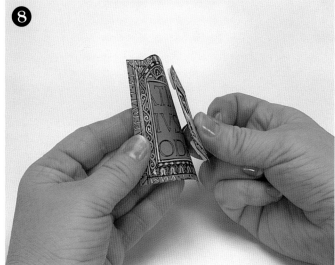

7. Adhere Small Frame to Face

Position the small frame over the David image so most of it can be seen through the window, and adhere with double-stick dots. Trim away all of the excess around the face.

8. Adhere Small Frame to Large Frame

Adhere the David image and small frame to the front of the large frame with double-stick dots.

9. Add Dots

Place more double-stick dots on the back of the frame.

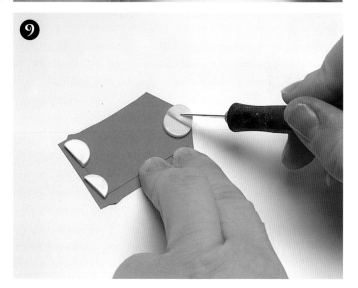

NOTE: To adhere small areas, try cutting double-stick dots into smaller pieces with craft scissors.

10. Adhere to Greeting Card

Fasten the framed face to the front of a folded blue greeting card, leaving room at the bottom for a special message if desired.

IN THE MAIL

blank postage paper is available at many stamp and scrapbook stores. Or, try making your own by using a sewing machine without thread to perforate the paper. I love this little big head stamp. I think it's perfect for Father's Day!

What you'll Need

Stamp*

- Little big head stamp

Materials

- Perforated stamp paper
- Folded dark blue greeting card
- Black dye ink
- Dye ink, various bright colors
- Markers
- Gel pens
- Eclipse tape
- Stiff brush
- Double-stick tape
- Craft knife

See Resource Guide for stamp credits.

TIP

With simple masking, create a thin white border around the image for a professional postage look.

1. Ink and Stamp Image
Ink the stamp with black dye ink and stamp several times onto perforated stamp paper. Stamp the image onto Eclipse tape, and use a craft knife to cut out the outline of the image to make a mask. Apply the mask over three of the stamped images on the postal stamp.

2. Apply Dye
Apply various colors of dye ink with a stiff brush. Next, remove the mask and color in the stamped images with markers (I used Galaxy brand) and gel pens.

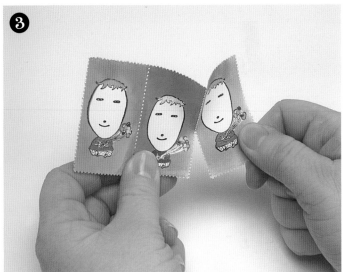

3. Separate Stamps
Tear the stamp paper apart at the perforations.

4. Adhere to Greeting Card
Cut pieces of double-stick tape to fit the back of each stamp and adhere diagonally from top-left to bottom-right onto the folded dark blue greeting card.

CELEBRATION OF SUMMER

i love these real pewter stickers, which are fairly new on the market. They come in a variety of shapes and designs. For this card, I uses inks to color in the fancy embellishments, but you may also prefer the pewter's natural finish. The 100% pewter stickers are soft and bendable, and they can be cut to size with craft scissors. Why not have a family reunion, summer solstice celebration or Independence day grill-out? The beauty of this card is that you can color coordinate it for any occasion.

TIP

This technique also works with foil stickers.

What you'll Need

Materials

- 6 pieces of decorative cardstock
- Folded tan greeting card
- Red and green solvent ink
- 2" (5cm) square pewter sticker
- Cosmetic sponge
- Craft scissors
- Double-stick tape
- Paper towels

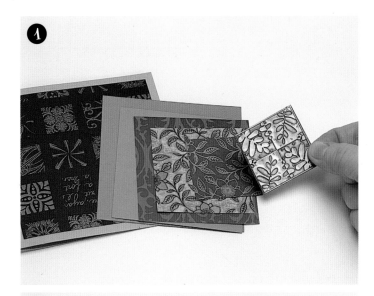

1. Cut Out Decorative Cardstock

Cut six pieces of decorative cardstock into squares of descending size. The sizes in this project are as follows: 5" x 5" (13cm x 13cm), 4½" x 4½" (11cm x 11cm), 4" x 4" (10cm x 10cm), 3½" x 3½" (9cm x 9cm), 3" x 3" (8cm x 8cm), 2⅛" x 2⅛" (7cm x 7cm). The pewter sticker should measure 2" x 2" (5cm x 5cm), and the greeting card should measure 5½" x 5½" (14cm x14cm). Layer the decorative cardstock in descending order with the smallest square on top. Adhere all the layers together with double-stick tape.

2. Ink Pewter Sticker

Apply two colors of solvent ink to the pewter sticker. For this project, I used red and green.

3. Spread Ink

Spread the ink around with a cosmetic sponge, completely covering the sticker.

4. Remove Excess Ink

Blot the excess ink from the pewter stamp with a paper towel. Allow the ink to dry.

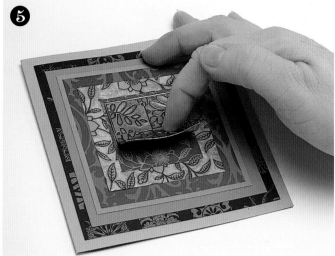

5. Adhere to Greeting Card

Using double-stick tape, adhere the layered cardstock to the greeting card. Next, adhere the pewter sticker to the cardstock.

More Bright Ideas

All the Leaves are Brown

Overlapping leaf stickers create the background on the pewter sticker in this card. Then, I used individual stickers in the center and along the edge as an accent. The pieces of the card are layered using double-stick dots to give it even more impact.

Toilettes

I applied a generous amount of dark green and blue solvent ink to the pewter sticker on this card. As a further embellishment, I also added a black satin ribbon trimmed in gold.

Daisies and Checks

Pewter stickers come in all shapes and sizes, as you can see in this card. Scrapbook stores have all sorts of coordinated papers where you can get pieces like these checks and stripes.

CARDS FOR FALL

fall is my favorite time of year. I love when the temperature drops and leaves turn beautiful shades of orange, brown and gold. It's the perfect time to roll up the sleeves of your favorite sweatshirt and get crafting! With a little ink, some colorful paper and a few stamps, you'll be amazed at how time flies. You may even get a jump on your winter holiday cards.

WARM UP THE SEASON WITH THESE FALL CARDS:

Spooky Sentiments 82 Gobbler Greetings 86 Fall Foliage 90

SPOOKY SENTIMENTS

halloween is my all-time favorite holiday! It is such a fun time, purely for tricks and treats (my friends know I'm a real joker). It's thrilling to create cards for this spooky holiday because they can be scary, humorous, cute or a mixture of all three!

TIP

To prevent your embossing powder from settling and sticking to the bottom of the jar, give it a shake before and after every use.

What you'll Need

Stamps*

* Shrine stamp
* Pumpkin head stamp

Materials

* Orange cardstock
* Black cardstock
* Black pigment ink
* Black permanent marker
* Silver pigment ink
* Embossing powder
* Embossing tool (heat gun)
* Markers
* Gel pens
* Double-stick dots
* Craft knife

See Resource Guide for stamp credits.

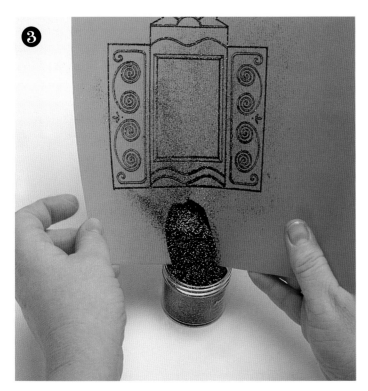

1. Ink and Stamp Frame Image
Ink the shrine stamp with black pigment ink and stamp onto orange cardstock. Quickly touch up the stamped image with a black permanent marker.

2. Apply Embossing Powder
Pour a generous amount of embossing powder over the stamped image. The powder will stick to the wet ink.

3. Save Excess Powder
Return the excess powder to the container.

4. Heat-Set Powder

Heat the stamped image with an embossing tool to set the powder in place.

5. Cut Out Center of Frame

Cut out the center of the shrine image with a craft knife. This becomes the frame for the card.

6. Color Frame

Color in portions of the frame with markers (I used Galaxy markers) and gel pens.

7. Ink and Stamp Halloween Image

Ink the pumpkin head stamp with silver pigment ink and stamp it onto black cardstock.

8. Adhere Image

Place the frame over the pumpkin head image and adhere with double-stick dots.

9. Make Stand

To make a stand for the frame, cut a triangle out of a scrap piece of black cardstock. Affix it to the back of the frame with double-stick dots.

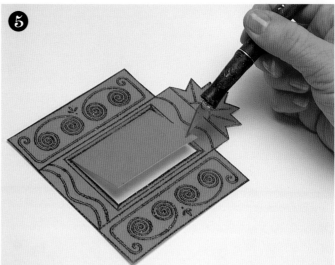

MORE BRIGHT IDEAS

Pumpkin Patch

This is another variation on the Halloween theme. I used double-stick dots to adhere the layers and to make the card three-dimensional.

GOBBLER GREETINGS

in this project, you get to carve your own turkey—turkey stamp, that is. Use the template provided to cut out the cute little gobbler. But beware! Carving can be addictive, and creating simple shapes from erasers can broaden your stamp collection. You'll quickly find that extra storage space in your craft room is something to be thankful for!

TIP

To deepen the warm fall tones in this card, I used an all-over vivid yellow paint as an overlay. This technique can be used with other colors as well. For instance, pink can be applied over blue and purple to brighten the look.

What you'll Need

Stamps*

- Hand-card turkey stamp (template on page 89)
- Leaf stamp

Materials

- Cream-colored cardstock
- Burgundy cardstock
- Folded tan greeting card
- Dye ink, various bright colors
- Black permanent marker
- Cosmetic sponge or stiff brush
- Pencil
- Eraser
- Carving tools
- Double-stick tape
- Craft scissors

*See Resource Guide for stamp credits.

1. Carve Turkey Stamp
Carve the individual pieces of the turkey stamp using the templates provided on page 89. (For instructions on how to carve your our own stamps, see page 17).

2. Ink and Stamp Turkey Feathers
Ink a leaf stamp with several colors of dye ink and stamp onto cream-colored cardstock to form the turkey's feathers.

3. Stamp Turkey Body
Ink the body stamp with brown dye ink and stamp over the feathers.

4. Stamp Turkey Head
Ink the turkey's head stamp with brown dye ink and stamp above the body.

5. Stamp Turkey Beak and Feet
Ink the turkey's beak and feet stamps with orange dye ink and stamp below the body.

6. Stamp Turkey Legs
Repeat the process with the turkey's legs.

7. Dot Turkey Eye
Dot the turkey's eye with a black permanent marker.

Templates are shown at 100%.

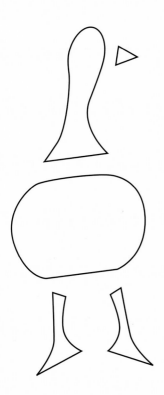

8. Cover with Yellow Ink
Cut the cardstock into an interesting geometric shape with craft scissors. Spread yellow dye ink over the entire turkey image with a cosmetic sponge.

9. Adhere Turkey Cardstock
Cut a piece of burgundy cardstock to the desired size and adhere to a folded greeting card with double-stick tape. Adhere the turkey card over the burgundy cardstock.

FALL FOLIAGE

acrylic tiles come in a myriad of shapes and sizes and can be found in most stamp supply stores. The clear tiles are lightweight enough to be used on cards. The ink selection is important on these tiles. Be sure to use a solvent ink or a pigment that can be dried with a heat gun. You may also want to try embossing the tiles for a metallic look.

What you'll Need

Stamp*

- Leaf stamp

Materials

- Thin decorative paper
- Folded light green greeting card
- Acrylic tile
- Metallic paint
- Copper paint pen
- Black solvent ink
- Stiff brush
- Double-stick tape
- Craft scissors

*See Resource Guide for stamp credits.

1. Paint Acrylic Tile
Use a stiff brush to cover an acrylic tile completely with metallic paint. (I used Halo Pink Gold paint by Lumiere.)

2. Apply Paint Pen
Fill in the unpainted areas with a copper paint pen. Allow to dry.

3. Remove Backing
Turn the acrylic tile onto the unpainted side and remove backing.

4. Ink and Stamp Leaf Image

Ink the leaf stamp with black solvent ink and randomly stamp it onto the unpainted side of the acrylic tile.

5. Reveal the Image

Continue stamping the leaves as desired. Allow to dry. The metallic paint shows through the stamped, unpainted side of the tile brilliantly.

6. Affix Decorative Paper

Using double-stick tape, adhere a piece of thin, decorative paper to the front of a light green greeting card at the fold. Trim off the excess.

7. Adhere Acrylic Tile

Adhere the acrylic tile to the front of the greeting card over the decorative paper.

Option: Acrylic Tile Experiment

There are so many creative ways to use acrylic tiles for craft projects. Here's a quick and easy idea I think you'll enjoy. The frog-shaped acrylic tile is covered with delicate gold leaf, giving it a faux metallic finish. Once the tile is dry, add it to any greeting card for instant shine.

1. Remove Tile Backing
Remove the backing from the frog-shaped acrylic tile.

2. Add Glaze
Using your finger, spread adhesive glaze on the frog piece.

3. Adhere Tile to Gold Leaf
Stick the adhesive side of the frog piece to gold leaf and allow to dry. (I used foil in this project, but tissue paper works just as well.)

4. Remove Excess Gold Leaf
Peel away the gold leaf and brush off any excess with a soft brush.

5. Fill with Paint Pen
Fill in any spaces with a gold paint pen.

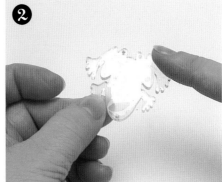

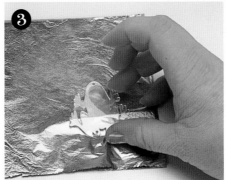

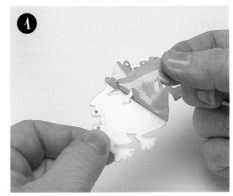

TIP

Use a full, soft brush to dust off the excess foil. A brush that is too stiff may remove too much foil and leave a scratchy appearance.

CARDS FOR TIMELESS OCCASIONS

many special occasions celebrated throughout the year are not marked by a particular season. Birthdays, anniversaries and housewarming parties are just a few of the many events that will keep you busy making cards all year long. Add a personal touch by decorating an animal-lover's card with a paw-print stamp, or embellish a history buff's card with vintage images. If you can dream it, you can make it. That, to me, is by far the best part about card-making.

SPREAD JOY YEAR-ROUND WITH THESE TIMELESS OCCASION CARDS:

Tiny Dancer 96 I Do 100 Bundle of Joy 104 Sweet Celebration 108 Comfy and Cozy 112

Cocktails, Anyone? 116 Home Sweet Home 120

TINY DANCER

this is a great card for a girly-girl party, be it a birthday, shower or other special occasion. Pink and white are the ultimate feminine color combination, although any pastel colors will work just as well.

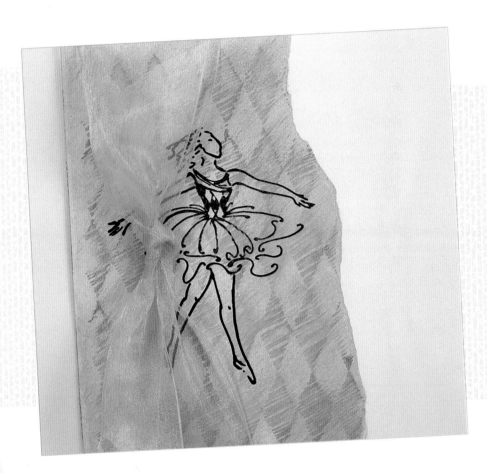

TIP

Use Eclipse tape to mask off the right side of the card in an uneven line. This will give the illusion of torn paper. This technique is also used in the "A Mother's Love" card on page 66.

What you'll Need

Stamps*

* Harlequin pattern stamp
* Ballerina stamp

Materials

* Folded white greeting card
* Light pink and dark pink
  pigment ink
* Black solvent ink
* Eclipse tape
* Light pink ribbon
* Stiff brush
* Craft scissors

See Resource Guide for stamp credits.

1. Mask Greeting Card
Use torn Eclipse tape to mask the outer edges of a folded white
greeting card. Apply a generous amount of light pink pigment ink
to the card.

2. Texturize Ink
While the ink is still wet, rub a stiff brush over the ink to texturize it.
Allow the card to dry completely.

3. Add More Color
Repeat the process, applying dark pink pigment ink over the light
pink layer.

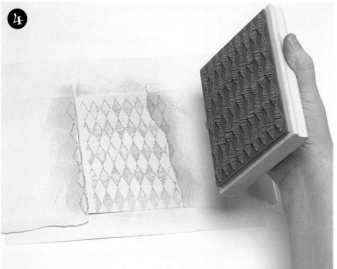

4. Ink and Stamp Harlequin Image
Ink a large harlequin patterned stamp with dark pink pigment ink and stamp over the greeting card.

5. Soften Image
To create a soft look, smear the image with your finger.

6. Ink and Stamp Ballerina Image
Ink a ballerina stamp with black solvent ink and stamp over the harlequin pattern.

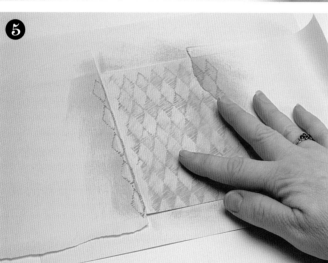

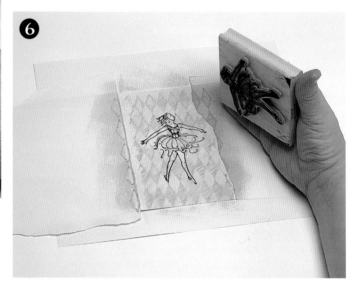

7. Remove Mask

Remove the mask of Eclipse tape and allow to dry.

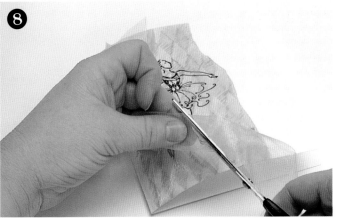

8. Add Ribbon

Fasten a light pink ribbon to the front of the card and tie it in a bow. Cut the ribbon edges at an angle for a decorative look.

More Bright Ideas

Marshmallow Bunny

Before the decorative images were stamped onto the background, masks were applied to the marshmallow bunny image and the right side of the card. When the masks were removed, these areas remained unstamped. This creates a layered appearance.

I DO

When we think of wedding cards, we typically visualize the traditional white-on-white color scheme. But what about the nontraditional couple? Colorful weddings are becoming more and more popular today, and a splash of color will make an ordinary card bright and beautiful—just like the happy couple!

TIP

To make a fancy greeting card like this one, paint a piece of white cardstock with a sandy paint. Then, add an iridescent interference paint over the sandy paint to pearlize it. Add more interference paint to pearlize again. Score the card down the middle with a stylus or the back of a craft knife and apply the stamped image as desired.

What you'll Need

Stamps*

- Bride and groom stamp

Materials

- White cardstock
- Folded iridescent greeting card (see tip on page 100)
- Black dye ink
- Pearlized paint
- Silver paint pen
- Glitter
- Decorative ribbon
- Pewter sticker
- Double-stick tape
- Craft scissors
- Cosmetic sponge
- Paintbrush
- Brayer (optional)

See Resource Guide for stamp credits.

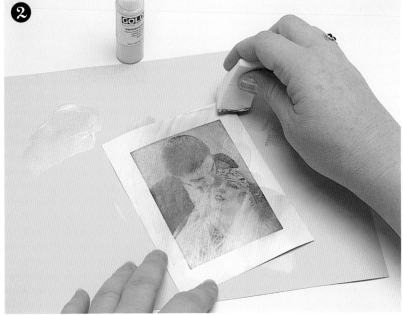

1. Ink and Stamp
Bride and Groom Image

Ink the bride and groom image with black dye ink. Stamp onto a piece of white cardstock.

NOTE: When inking a large stamp such as this, use a brayer to distribute the ink more evenly.

---

2. Apply Paint

Spread pearlized paint over the stamped image with a cosmetic sponge.

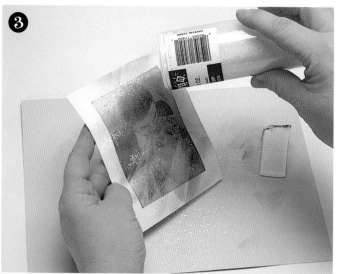

3. Apply Glitter

Add glitter to the wet paint and dust off the excess. Allow to dry.

4. Outline Edges

Trim the edges of the cardstock right up to the edge of the stamped image. Outline the edges with a silver paint pen.

5. Add Ribbon and Adhere to Greeting Card

With double-stick tape, adhere the cardstock and a decorative ribbon to a folded silver greeting card. Finally, adhere a pewter sticker over the ribbon.

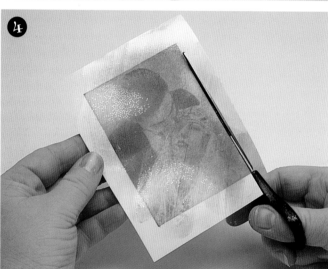

MORE BRIGHT IDEAS

Family Matters

This card is an example of how glitter can be a subtle embellishment. Adhere the image to a glossy greeting card in a soft shade of turquoise, and attach a decorative ribbon for a charming touch.

Stars in Your Eyes

A simple, white greeting becomes a sparkling masterpiece just by adding glitter to a simple face stamp. Black ribbon and decorative paper also add visual appeal.

BUNDLE OF JOY

Pastel pink or baby blue, a handmade baby shower invitation will surely make mommy and her guests smile. With the help of a box template, this quick and easy card looks like it took all day to make. I used a simple envelope template to make an all-in-one look. It can be used for other occasions, too. Make several of these at a time to keep ahead of your card-making for every occasion.

TIP

Use yellow cardstock and green ink for a gender-neutral invitation.

What you'll Need

Stamps*

- Baby bottle stamp
- "You're Invited" stamp
- Little gift stamp

Materials

- Box template (page 107)
- Pink or blue cardstock
- White cardstock
- Dye inks, various colors
- Pink or blue paint pen
- Pencil
- Stylus
- Double-stick tape
- Craft scissors

See Resource Guide for stamp credits.

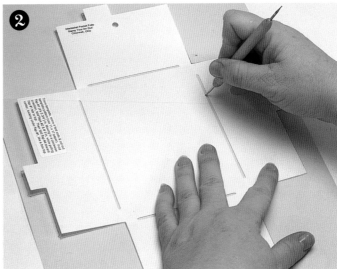

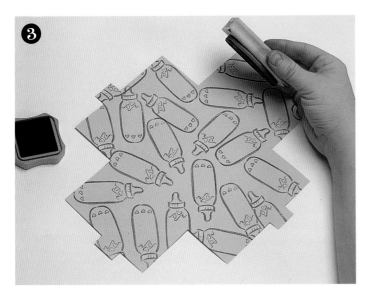

1. Cut Out Template

Enlarge and cut out the box template on page 107. Trace the template with a pencil on the pink or blue cardstock.

2. Score and Cut Box

Score with a stylus where the folds will be, and cut out the box with craft scissors.

3. Ink and Stamp Bottle Image

Ink the baby bottle stamp with colored dye ink and stamp randomly onto the box. Set aside.

4. Decorate Inside of Card
Cut out a piece of white cardstock to the size of the inside of the box, about 5½" x 4¼" (14cm x 10.8cm). Ink the "You're Invited," baby bottle and little gift stamps with various colored dye inks and stamp onto the white cardstock. Outline the edges with a pink or blue paint pen.

5. Adhere Cardstock to Inside of Box
Adhere the white cardstock to the inside back panel of the box with double-stick tape.

6. Close Box
To close the box, fold the flaps inward beginning with the top and bottom, then the left and right. Tuck the flaps under to secure.

Enlarge template to 167%.

SWEET CELEBRATION

translucent vellum is still the easiest way to add elegance to any card. The variety of colors and patterns available in most craft stores makes it easy to create the ultimate individual look. Choose colors and prints that remind you of the birthday girl or boy and find wrapping paper to coordinate!

What you'll Need

Stamps*

- "Happy Birthday" stamp
- Birthday cake stamp

Materials

- 2 pieces of decorative paper
- Turquoise vellum
- Folded white greeting card
- Silver dye ink
- Purple dye ink
- Double-stick tape
- Craft scissors

*See Resource Guide for stamp credits.

1. Ink and Stamp "Happy Birthday"
Ink the "Happy Birthday" stamp with purple dye ink and stamp randomly onto turquoise Xyroned vellum. (Running vellum through a Xyron machine will add a sticky coating to one side.)

2. Tear Vellum
Tear the edges of the stamped vellum on both sides.

3. Adhere Decorative Paper
Using double-stick tape, adhere a 3" (7.6cm) square piece of decorative paper diagonally onto the front of a folded white greeting card.

4. Adhere Vellum to Greeting Card
Cover the entire front of the greeting card with the stamped vellum.

5. Ink Cake Image
Ink a birthday cake stamp with silver dye ink.

NOTE: When using a triple stamp pad as shown, ink only one cake image.

6. Stamp Cake Image onto Decorative Paper
Cut out another square of decorative paper measuring 2" (5cm) square. Stamp the cake image in the center of the square.

7. Adhere Decorative Paper to Card
Using double-stick tape, adhere the small square over the vellum on the greeting card, positioning it diagonally over the larger square. Trim the bottom of the card as necessary.

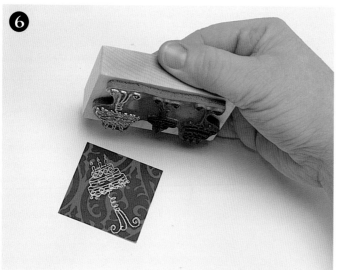

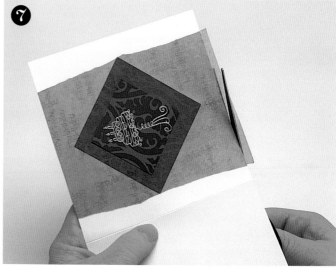

MORE BRIGHT IDEAS

Beautiful Greenery

The layered squares of paper in this card add such elegance, your loved ones will never know how easy it is to make. Choose decorative paper in matching shades, or use the scrap paper you have saved from other projects.

Colors of Fall

Using paper with different patterns and textures will make your cards more interesting and fun. Vary the shapes of the paper as well. Here, the circle among all the squares really sets off the simple leaf.

COMFY AND COZY

masking can be so impressive when done well—and Eclipse tape makes it super simple. Look for stamps with open areas, like this overstuffed couch, so you can use all your favorite small designs to decorate the fabric.

TIP

Creating a plaid pattern with a word stamp is easy. Stamp the words so they run both horizontally and vertically and use varying amounts of ink on the stamp to create light and dark lines.

What you'll Need

Stamps*

- Comfy chair stamp
- "Thank You" stamp

Materials

- Folded white greeting card
- Dye ink, various bright colors
- Black solvent ink
- Orange paint pen
- Eclipse tape
- Craft knife

*See Resource Guide for stamp credits.

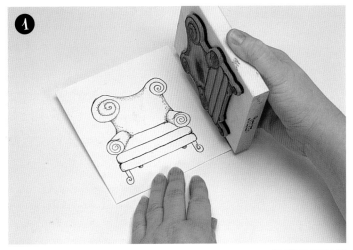

1. Ink and Stamp Chair Image

Ink the comfy chair stamp with black solvent ink and stamp onto a folded white greeting card.

2. Roll Eclipse Tape Over Stamp

Ink the stamp again and roll Eclipse tape over it to transfer the image.

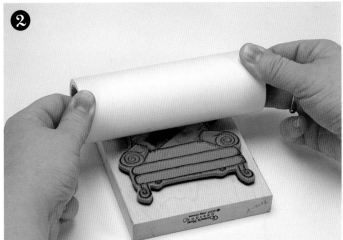

3. Cut Out Chair Image

Cut out the chair image from the Eclipse tape with a craft knife. You will be left with an outline of the chair, which will be your mortise mask. (For more information on masking, see page 19.)

NOTE: Save the chair cut-out to use as a regular mask on another card.

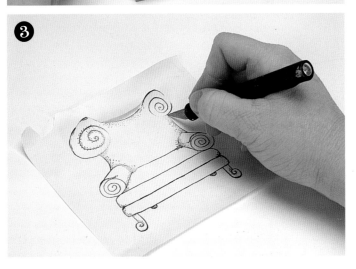

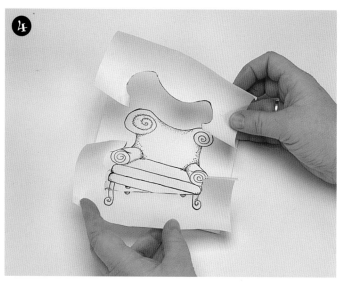

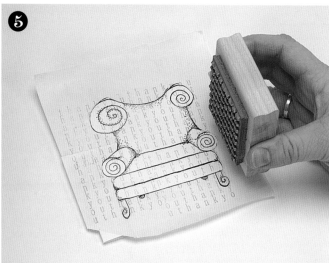

4. Cut Mask in Two Pieces
Cut the mortise mask into two pieces. This will make it easier to work with.

5. Apply Mask and Stamp "Thank You"
Apply the mask around the chair image on the greeting card. Ink the "Thank You" stamp with various colors of dye ink and stamp it horizontally and vertically onto the greeting card. Remove the mask.

6. Mask Inside of Greeting Card
Cut out another piece of Eclipse tape and stick it to the inside of the greeting card, masking all but the far right edge.

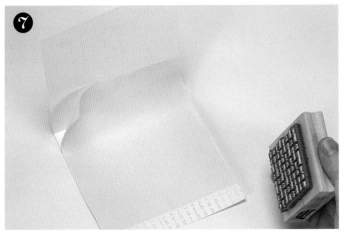

7. Ink and Stamp "Thank You"

Ink the "Thank You" stamp with various colors of dye ink and stamp the inside edge of the greeting card. Remove the mask and trim the front of the greeting card along the right-hand side so that the inside edge is visable.

8. Color Chair Feet

Color the feet of the chair with an orange paint pen.

More Bright Ideas

Have a Seat

Use the regular and mortise chair masks to create cards with different patterns and colors on the chair and walls. If you plan to apply the masks over and over, I suggest using a heavier paper, as it will hold up to more wear and tear.

COCKTAILS, ANYONE?

dusting metal pigments over wet pigment ink can give a card an elegant, matte metal look. When combined with an array of whimsical stamps, this card is the perfect mix of sophistication and fun. Metal pigments are a bit more difficult to find, but well worth the effort. They truly look like foil leaf and are usable with any type of pigment ink.

TIP

Keep the metal dust under control with a lint roller. Simply roll over the metallic area of the finished card to pick up any remaining dust. I use lint rollers for cleaning up glitter and other dry pigments as well.

What you'll Need

Stamps*

- Cocktails stamp
- Filler drink stamp

Materials

- Green cardstock
- Silver cardstock
- Folded silver greeting card
- Black pigment ink
- Gold pigment powder
- Spray fixative
- Paper cord
- Soft brush
- Pencil
- Double-stick tape
- Craft scissors

*See Resource Guide for stamp credits.

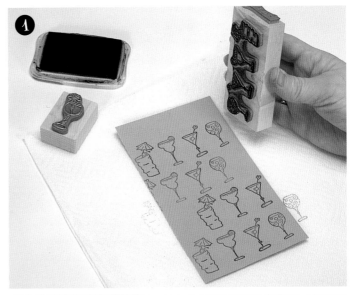

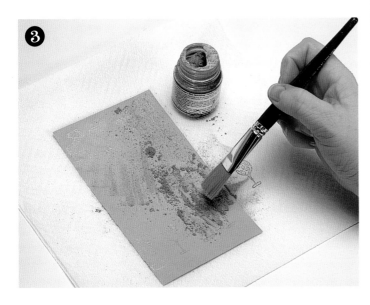

1. Ink and Stamp Cocktails
Ink the cocktails stamp with black pigment ink and stamp it onto green cardstock.

2. Fill in Blank Spaces
Use a filler drink stamp to stamp in the blank spaces.

3. Apply Pigment Powder
Use a soft brush to dust the card with gold pigment powder. The powder will adhere to the wet ink.

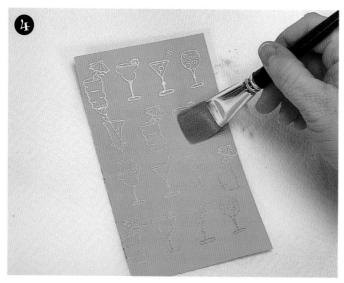

4. Remove Excess Powder
Wipe away the excess powder.

5. Apply Fixative
Spray the entire card with fixative (I used Krylon Spray Workable Fixative) to prevent smudging and protect the card from the elements.

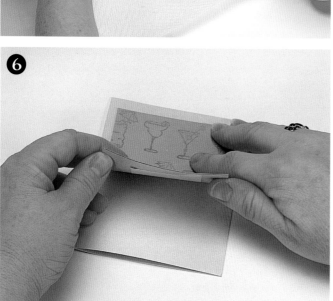

6. Adhere Cardstock to Greeting Card
Trim the green cardstock and adhere to the front of a folded silver greeting card with double-stick tape.

7. Stamp and Adhere Image
Stamp one of the images from the cocktails stamp onto a small scrap of green cardstock. Trim around the edges of the image and adhere it to a slightly larger square of silver cardstock with double-stick tape. Trim again as needed.

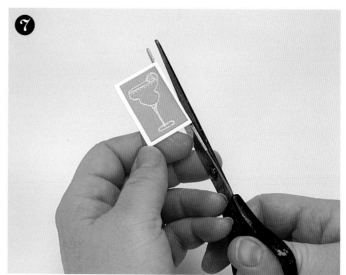

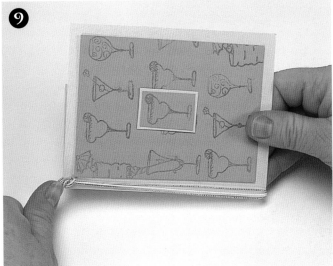

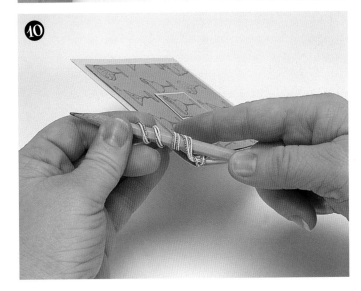

8. Adhere Silver Cardstock
Adhere the small square of silver cardstock to the center of the green cardstock.

9. Add Cord
Add a paper cord to the card and knot at the top.

10. Curl Cord Ends
Curl the ends of the cord with a pencil.

HOME SWEET HOME

When you need to whip up a quick housewarming or hostess card, this is the design for you. Choose stamps with crisp geometric edges to keep this card simple. These house stamps are just the ticket! With a little creative cutting, the colors seem to shine right through the windows.

TIP

To prevent light colors from getting muddy, use the dye stamp pads in order from lightest to darkest.

What you'll Need

Stamps*

- House stamp
- "Party" stamp

Materials

- Folded white greeting card
- Black solvent ink
- Dye ink, various bright colors
- Black permanent marker
- Eclipse tape
- Craft knife
- Ruler

*See Resource Guide for stamp credits.

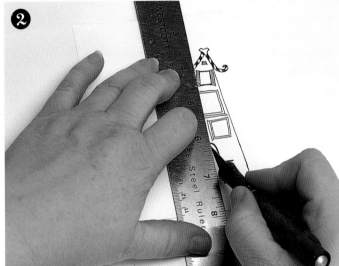

1. Ink and Stamp House Image

Ink the house stamp with black solvent ink and stamp the image onto the right-hand edge of a folded white greeting card.

2. Cut Through House

Open the card and lay it out flat. Using the straight edge of the ruler and a craft knife, cut a border through the house, taking care not to detatch the house from the front of the card.

3. Cut Out Windows and Door

Cut out the windows, door and around the right side of the house. The house becomes the right-hand border of the card.

4. Outline Edges

Outline the edges of the house image with black permanent marker.

5. Mask Inside of Card and Stamp with Inkpads

Mask off the inside of the card with Eclipse tape, exposing only the far right edge. Stamp the edge with dye inkpads in varying colors. Remove the mask and allow the ink to dry.

6. Ink and Stamp "Party"

Mask off the front of the card, exposing only the bottom edge. Ink the "Party" stamp with brightly colored dye inks and stamp along the bottom of the card.

7. Add Finishing Touch

To finish the card, use a ruler and black permanent marker to draw a line above the "Party" stamps.

More Bright Ideas

Cut It Out

Stamping the gift image at playful angles makes for a terrific edge for the cut-out. I created the colored background first, then stamped the gift boxes and colored them to complement the background that shows through.

'Tis the Season

Making fancy edges along the side of a card is much easier than it looks. Here, I stamped red and green inkpads and silver stars on the inside edge and colored in the house stamp with markers.

Resources

Stamp Suppliers

American Art Stamp
3870 Del Amo Blvd.
Suite 501
Torrance, CA 90503
Phone: (310) 371-6593
Fax: (310) 371-5545
• Stamps used: Present; Little gift; "You're Invited"; Triple hearts; Lamps; Chinese lantern; Dress; "Happy Valentine's Day"; Birthday cake; "Happy Birthday"; Cocktails; "Party"

Art Gone Wild
3110 Payne Ave.
Cleveland, OH 44114
Phone: (800) 945-3980
Fax: (888) 401-2979
www.agwstamps.com
• Stamps used: Box template

DeNami Design
P.O. Box 5617
Kent, WA 98064
Phone: (253) 437-1626
Fax: (253) 437-1627
www.denamidesign.com
• Stamps used: Baby bottle

Earth Tone Images
P.O. Box 814
Havertown, PA 19083
Phone: (610) 645-6500
Fax: (610) 645-9631
www.earthtoneimages.com
• Stamps used: Handprint

JudiKins
17832 S. Hobart Blvd.
Gardena, CA 90248
Phone: (310) 515-1115
Fax: (310) 323-6619
• Stamps used: Leaves and butterfly; Swirl: Funky swirl; Fall leaves; Star; Harlequin background; Ballerina; Nile flowers stained glass; Primitive flower; Minstrel; Retro circle; Mini squares; Polka dots

paula best and co.
507 Trail Dr.
Moss Landing, CA 95039
Phone: (831) 632-0587
www.paulabest.com
• Stamps used: Menorah

Postmodern Design
P.O. Box 720416
Norman, OK 73070
Postmoderndesign@aol.com
• Stamps used: David; Boy and girl; Molly's face

Post Script Studio/Carmen's Veranda
P.O. Box 1539
Placentia, CA 92871
Fax: (714) 528-4529
www.postscriptstudio.com
postscriptstudio@msn.com
• Stamps used: Shrine; Marshmallow bunny

River City Rubber Works
5555 S. Meridian
Wichita, KS 67217
Phone: (877) 735-2276
Fax: (316) 529-8940
www.rivercityrubberworks.com
• Stamps used: Leaf

Rubbermoon
P.O. Box 3258
Hayden Lake, ID 83835
www.rubbermoon.com
rubbermoon@nidlink.com
• Stamps used: Pumpkin head; Pumpkins; House; Christmas house; Little bird

Stamper's Anonymous
Williamsburg Square
25967 Detroit Rd.
Cleveland, OH 44145
Phone: (440) 250-9112
Fax: (440) 250-9117
www.stampersanonymous.com
• Stamps used: Large frame stamp; Small frame stamp

Stampotique
9822 North 7th St.
Suite 7
Phoenix, AZ 85020
Phone: (602) 862-0237
Fax: (602) 862-0238
www.stampotique.com
• Stamps used: Little big head; Comfy chair; "Thank You"

Other Suppliers

American Crafts
165 N. 1330 W. B3
Orem, UT 84057
Phone: (800) 879-5185
Fax: (801) 226-5086
www.americancrafts.com
• Galaxy markers and gel pens

Amy's Magic Leaf
173 Main St.
West Leechburg, PA 15656
Phone: (724) 845-1748
• Paper Foil Ephemera

Coffee Break Design
P.O. Box 34281
Indianapolis, IN 46234
Fax: (800) 229-1824
• Eyelets

Colorbox
P.O. Box 98
Anacortes, WA 98821
Phone: (800) 448-4862
www.clearsnap.com
• Inks

Envelopes Please
9685 Kenwood Rd
Cincinnati OH 45242
Phone: (513) 793-4558
www.stampawayusa.com
• Templates

Golden Paints
188 Bell Road
New Berlin, NY 13411
Phone: (607) 847-6154
www.goldenpaints.com
• Acrylic paints

Jacquard
540 Lake Cook Rd.
Suite 160
Deerfield, IL 60015
Phone: (800) 442-0455
Fax: (847) 945-8704
www.jacquard.com
e-mail: jacquard@jacquard.com
• PearlEx powdered pigments

Magenta
2275 Bombardier
Sainte-Julie
QC Canada J3E 2J9
Phone: (450) 922-5253
www.magentastyle.com
• Pewter stickers, printed papers

Marvy Uchida
Phone: (800) 541-5877
www.uchida.com
• Inks

On the Surface
P.O. Box 8026
Wilmette, IL 60091
Phone: (847)675-2521
• Threads and fibers

Really Reasonable Ribbon
P.O. Box 199
Sugar Loaf, NY 10981
Phone: (845) 469-3821
www.reasonableribbon.com
• Ribbons

Speedball Art Products Company
2226 Speedball Rd.
Statesville, NC 28677
Phone: (800) 898-7224
Fax: (704) 838-1472
www.speedballart.com
• Carving supplies

Suzi Finer Artworks & Artware
238 S. Robertson Blvd
Beverly Hills, CA 90211
Phone: (310) 360-1800
Fax: (310) 360-1801
www.suzifiner.com
e-mail: suzi@suzifiner.com
• Pewter stickers

Tsukineko, Inc
17640 N.E. 65th St.
Redmond, WA 98052
Phone: (800) 769-6633
Fax: (425) 883-7418
www.tsukineko.com
e-mail: sales@tsukineko.com
• Inks

USArtquest
7800 Ann Arbor
Grass Lake, MI 49240
Phone: (517) 522-6225
www.usartquest.com
• Pinata inks

Index

A Mother's Love, 66
accessories, 11
acetate, 12, 27
acrylic paint, 30
acrylic tiles, 90, 93
All the Leaves are Brown, 78

baby, 104
ballpoint pen, 16
beads, 11
Beautiful Greenery, 111
Birthday, 96, 108
bone folder, 10, 16
box template, 104, 107
brayer, 10
bulk cards, 24
Bundle of Joy, 104
bunny template, 61
Butterfly in the Sky, 33

cardstock, 12
carving, 17
carving tools. 17
Celebration of Summer, 76
Christmas Box, 24
cleaning, 15
Cocktails, Anyone?, 116
colored pencils, 35
Colors of Fall, 111
Comfy and Cozy, 112
confetti, 45
cord, 11, 33, 119
cosmetic sponge, 77, 101
craft knife, 10, 14, 16
craft scissors, 10

crayons, 11
Cross my Heart, 42

Daisies and Checks, 79
decorative paper, 53, 77, 92, 109, 111
Diamond Glaze, 11
double-stick dots, 73, 85
double-stick tape, 10
dye ink, 13, 40, 46

Easter, 56
Easter egg template, 61
Eclipse tape, 47, 64, 75, 96, 97, 113, 114
Embellishments, 11
embossing powder, 11, 39, 83
embossing tool, 11, 39, 84
Encore, 38
Eraser, 17

Facing the Future, 70
Fall Foliage, 90
Family Matters, 103
Father's Day, 74
fixative, 118
foil stickers, 76

Galaxy markers, 66, 67, 70, 71, 75, 84
gel pens, 70, 71, 75
glaze, 93
Glazed Metallics, 38
Glitter, 28, 45, 102, 103
Gobbler Greetings, 86
gold leaf, 93
graduation, 70

Halloween, 82
Halo Pink Gold, 91
Hanukkah, 30
Have a Seat, 115
heart pocket template, 45
heart template, 44
Hearts of Gold, 46
Home Sweet Home, 120

I Do, 100
In the Mail, 74
inking large stamps, 15
inks, 13
interference paint, 100

Joseph's Coat, 34

Krylon, 118

Leaving an Impression, 33
Light the Menorah, 30
lint roller, 116
Lumiere, 91

Mardi Gras, 52
Marshmallow Bunny, 99
Masking, 47, 62, 64, 75, 96, 97, 99, 112, 114
metallic paint, 33
Midas' Golden Touch, 49
mortise mask, 112, 113

New Year, 34

overlay, 86

paint pen, 91, 93, 115

Index

paper, 12
paper clip, 16
Party Gras!, 52
pearlized paint, 101
Peekaboo Bunny, 56
permanent ink (see solvent ink), 13
permanent marker, 37
pewter stickers, 76, 102
pigment ink, 13, 38, 116
pigment powder, 48, 116, 117
pop-up card, 16
postage paper, 74
powdered pigments, 11
Pumpkin Patch, 85

resist method, 34
ribbon, 33, 79, 103
rubber brayer, 15
ruler, holding a, 14

sandy paint, 100
scoring, 16, 53, 57
scoring tool, 43
shower, 96
silver paint pen, 32
solvent ink, 13
sponge, 46
Spooky Sentiments, 82
Stamps, 12
Stars in Your Eyes, 103
stiff paint brush, 31, 46
stylus, 16
summer solstice, 76
Sunbonnets in Spring, 62
Sweet Celebration, 108

Thanksgiving, 86
thread, 11
Tie-Dyed Flowers, 49
Tiny Dancer, 96
Toilettes, 79
torn edges, 32, 49, 109
translucent paper (see vellum)
tri-fold card, 16, 56
turkey template, 89

Valentine's Day, 42
vellum, 12, 43, 108

water-soluble crayons, 11
wedding, 100
window plastic, 12

Xyroned vellum, 109

GET CREATIVE WITH NORTH LIGHT BOOKS

The Essential Guide to Handmade Books

Gabrielle Fox teaches you how to create your own handmade books—one-of-a-kind art pieces that go beyond the standard definition of what a "book" can be. You'll find 11 projects inside. Each one builds upon the next, just as your skills increase. This beginner-friendly progression ensures that you're well prepared to experiment, play and design your own unique handmade books.

ISBN 1-58180-019-3, paperback, 128 pages, #31652-K

The Big Book of Greeting Cards

This book presents a variety of fun, festive and stylish ideas for making cards perfect for any occasion. Discover more than 40 step-by-step projects using a wide range of techniques including rubber stamping, stenciling, quilling and embroidery.

ISBN 1-58180-323-0, paperback, 144 pages, #32287-K

How to Be Creative if You Never Thought You Could

Let Tera Leigh act as your personal craft guide and motivator. She'll help you discover just how creative you really are. You'll explore eight exciting crafts through 16 fun, fabulous projects, including rubber stamping, bookmaking, papermaking, collage, decorative painting and more. Tera prefaces each new activity with insightful essays and encouraging advice.

ISBN 1-58180-293-5, paperback, 128 pages, #32170-K

Stenciling & Embossing Greeting Cards

Judy Barker introduces you to the basics of stenciling and embossing attractive greeting cards. You'll also learn how to embellish them with foil, polymer clay, shrink plastic and more. It's everything you need to make one-of-a-kind cards for family and friends alike.

ISBN 0-89134-997-9, paperback, 128 pages, #31613-K

Greeting Card Magic with Rubber Stamps

Discover great new tricks for creating extra-special greeting cards! Pick up your stamp, follow along with the illustrated, step-by-step instructions inside, and ta da! You'll amaze everyone (including yourself!) with your beautiful and original creations.

ISBN 0-89134-979-0, paperback, 128 pages, #31521-K

These and other fine North Light titles are available from your local art & craft retailer, bookstore, online supplier or by calling 1-800-448-0915.